This Way

ALGARVE

Ken Bernstein

CONTENTS

This Way Algarve

A Place in the Sun

For years, nobody in the rest of Europe seemed to know where the Algarve was, much less how to pronounce it. The image was Mediterranean, and the travel agents didn't lift a finger to correct the slight misapprehension. After all, the atmosphere of lazy beaches, olive groves and blinding white houses looked pretty much the same whether the body of water was the Med or the Atlantic. Then there was the Portuguese connection. Until the nation's dictatorship was overthrown in 1974's "carnation revolution", the Algarve was promoted as a place in limbo—vaguely somewhere in southern Europe.

Now that Portugal is a democracy in Europe's mainstream, they provide maps. And one of the selling points is the fact that, unlike many places in the Mediterranean, the Algarve's Atlantic beaches are paragons of purity. Dozens of them have been awarded the coveted blue flags of approval by the European Union. No more limbo for Portugal's prime tourist destination.

Foreigners in significant numbers discovered the Algarve in the 1960s. The first to appreciate the region's climate, scenery and way of life were the English, who made a big impression on the locals. That's why Algarvians tend to call all foreigners, no matter where they come from, "Ingleses".

Map Reading

The area of the Algarve, Portugal's southernmost province, is about the same as the state of Delaware, or twice the size of Luxembourg. From east to west it stretches from the Guadiana River (the border with Spain) to the cliffs of Cape St. Vincent, jutting into the Atlantic in the direction of the next landfall—the south-east coast of the United States. Between these boundaries, the Algarve looks south onto a 100-mile (160-km) Atlantic coastline of beaches for all tastes—from endless strands of the softest white sand to tiny sun-toasted coves tucked between awesome rock formations. Inland, fertile orchards provide the citrus fruit, olives, figs and almonds that will delight you, 3

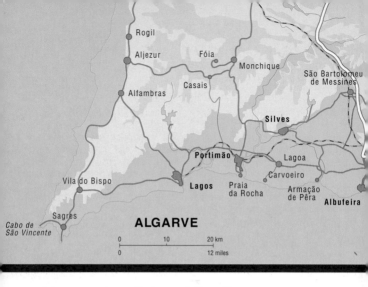

and the scenery is as alluring as almond blossom in January. The uplands beyond are covered with pines, eucalyptus, and the most enchanting wild flowers.

If you want to get away from it all, the direction to go is north—uphill—where scarcely a whiff of the tourist industry intrudes. Here the artisans keep alive the old skills—though the buyers, in fact, are tourists.

But along the southern coast the truth is that almost every sandy cove has spawned a resort, and some of them will make you wonder what ever happened to Portuguese moderation and good taste.

Two Faces

The beaches of the Algarve have a split personality. The sands of the eastern half, called the Sotavento (leeward) coast, are flat and expansive—so big that the happy sunbather may face a long trek to dip a toe in the water. The western half, called the Barlavento (windward) coast, comes under the influence of the open Atlantic, which has created eerie rock formations, caves and hidden coves. The nearer you get to Cape St. Vincent, the "end of the world" peninsula, the smaller and more secluded the beaches become. It all depends whether you're looking for a children's

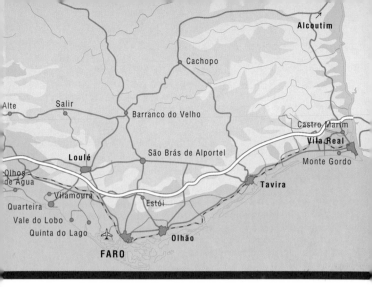

beach, a scuba site or a wind-surfers' rendezvous. Somewhere along the coast is the beach of your dreams.

3,000 Hours

The Portuguese are famous for their modesty, but they're not shy about enlisting statistics to prove that the Algarve is one of the sunniest resort areas in Europe. With 3,000 hours of sunshine per year, on average, you don't have to dodge the raindrops to brush up your tennis or golf. But you do have to take care not to overdo the broiling on the beach. When the sun goes down, the Algarve's nightlife is as cosmopolitan as its tourists—everything from karaoke sing-alongs to throbbing discos. There are three big casinos with sophisticated floor shows and gambling facilities. Or you might settle for a fish dinner overlooking the ocean and a folklore show, or the melancholy sound of the *fado,* the song of the Portuguese soul.

A Kettle of Fish

The brightly painted fishing boats on the beaches are not for show; they mean business. Fishing is a vital industry here, not only to feed the tourist legions but for export. Chances are the can of sardines stowed 5 in your kitchen cupboard at home originated in the Algarve (you probably didn't know how tasty are *fresh* sardines, a totally different kettle of fish).

The big ocean-going trawlers are moored at the serious fishing ports, like Olhão and Portimão, where the sound of the sea is a siren announcing the auction of a boatload of fish. The buyers jostle for a look; a captain's livelihood hangs on the results. His leathery face betraying no emotion beyond fatigue, the mariner goes home with a plastic bag in hand, containing a little something he set aside for tonight's *sopa de peixe*—fish soup.

Moorish Echoes

At the beginning of the 8th century, Muslim invaders from North Africa overran the Iberian peninsula. The Moors, as they were called, stayed here for five centuries, until the Christian Reconquest triumphed. They gave the Algarve its name—in Arabic, *Al Gharb,* meaning western land, for this was as far west as the known world went. The Moors also named towns like Albufeira and Almansil, Alcoutim and Alvor; many a village church is built on the ruins of a mosque. Their legacy is apparent everywhere in the region; you'll see it in the whitewashed villages with decorative chimneys, the water-wheels and the crops they irrigate, the superrich sweets in the pastry shops. Almost every village has its local speciality, if only at festivals—cakes, candies, puddings and pastries always based on the favourite local ingredients—sugar, egg, almonds and figs. And you can't miss the hint of Moorish roots in the impassive, swarthy faces of today's Algarve farmers and fishermen.

THE BEST SUNSET Whether you're looking for a memorable photo or a breath of poetry and romance, the Algarve offers great sunsets. Best of all is from the "Sacred Promontory", **Cape St. Vincent**: you can see the sun slide into the midst of several thousand miles of uninterrupted ocean. To put the dramatic cape itself into the picture, move south-eastward to Sagres.

Flashback

Unmonumental

The Portuguese, in any case, are given to understatement. So you'll hardly notice that most of the Algarve's major monuments of historical significance have been lost, one way or another. Any that survived typhoons, pirate raids and full-scale wars were doomed to be destroyed in the most devastating earthquake to hit 18th-century Europe. Thus history surrounds you in less triumphal forms: a Roman hot spring, an Arabic inscription, a medieval turret.

The Phoenicians were the first foreign influence on the Algarve, establishing trading posts in, for instance, what is now Faro. But they were business travellers, not colonists, and left little trace. Their successors were Celts, Iberians, Greeks, and Carthaginians, who ruled the coast until the arrival of the Romans in the 3rd century BC. Thus the Algarve became part of the province of Lusitania.

Under the Romans

The Roman empire left little that is exceptional in the Algarve—most of the inscribed stones, chipped statues and pots would hardly rate a glance in the world's leading museums. A big, lovely mosaic of a bearded god of the sea was found in the middle of Faro, and a sunken bath with mosaics of fish embellishes the ruins of a suburban villa. More may still be hidden. On the border between the ancient provinces of Lusitania and Baetica (later Portugal and Spain), the Romans built serious fortifications at Castro Marim.

Nothing special—but the Romans are remembered for the culture they brought, rather than for artefacts. The Latin language, for a start, is the ancestor of modern Portuguese (and the related tongues of Spain and Italy). Roman engineers built roads and bridges. Roman agricultural experts introduced wheat, olives and grapes to local farmers.

Later, the Roman legions brought word of a new religion, Christianity. In the 4th century AD a bishop was installed in the Algarve. But by then the empire was in a tailspin and Europe was heading for the Dark Ages.

7

Armaçao de Pera is timeless, but a big resort complex now surrounds it.

The Islamic Tide

The Visigoths controlled the Algarve early in the 8th century when they were engulfed by the tide of Islam. The invaders came from North Africa, an overwhelming army of Berber troops sworn to spread the message of the Prophet Mohammed, to which they were newly converted themselves. Resistance was negligible, and within a few years the Moors controlled virtually all of the Iberian peninsula. In the Algarve, the new rulers built and fortified their capital, Xelb (now called Silves). The Moorish influence—in agriculture, architecture, art, and the attitudes of the people—can still be seen all over the Algarve. Xelb developed into a glittering centre of Arab commerce and culture, reputedly richer than Lisbon. Its fame was so widespread that Viking raiders arrived in AD 966 and sailed up the River Arade in an attempt to loot the place. They were turned back.

Reconquest

Expelling the Moors from the Algarve was an on-again, off-again struggle that lasted centuries. It enlisted the zeal of the Crusaders, who stopped off on their way to the Holy Land to seize Silves in a terrible battle in

8

1189. King Sancho I finally sent the victorious Crusaders packing because of their excesses in pillaging. Then he took the title "King of Portugal and Silves." This turned out to be premature, for the Muslims regained control of the battered city two years later. They were finally dislodged in a deadly siege towards the middle of the 13th century under King Alfonso III, son of Alfonso the Fat. The new title was "King of Portugal and the Algarve", which emphasized the province's remoteness from the rest of the country.

Age of Discovery

Portugal's King John the Bastard, who ruled from 1385 to 1433, married Philippa of Lancaster, daughter of John of Gaunt. They had six sons, the most remarkable of whom came to be called Henry the Navigator. The prince's intellect, imagination and boldness produced one of history's truly heroic eras, the Age of Discovery. Little travelled himself, Henry mobilized an international team of specialists—astronomers, cartographers, geographers, mathematicians and naval architects—and installed them in a sort of think tank in the Algarve. The site of his "School of Navigation" was the Sacred Promontory at Sagres, the moody, windswept "end of the world". Prince Henry convinced his seamen that they could sail into the unknown and return quickly and safely in newly designed caravels, built in Lagos. Each expedition into the Atlantic and down the coast of Africa went a bit farther, bringing back new data to be incorporated on the maps.

By the time the visionary prince died in 1460, his scouts had sailed as far south as Sierra Leone. The momentum continued with the pioneering voyages of Vasco da Gama, who rounded the Cape of Good Hope and founded a colony in India. Brazil was claimed in 1500, and Portuguese traders soon settled in the Spice Islands, Ceylon and China. Portugal presided over the greatest overseas empire of its day.

Boy-King

Prince Sebastian, born in 1554, was left fatherless at the age of three. After a regency period, he was enthroned, aged 14, as King of Portugal. Nothing good was to come of his reign, except a persistent national dream. Dreamy is the word for Sebastian, who saw himself as a royal crusader. He raised an army and set forth from Lagos with more enthusiasm than aptitude, aiming to teach a lesson to the Muslims of North Africa. (An 9 enigmatic modern statue of the boy-king stands in the pedestrian zone of Lagos.) At Ksar el-Kebir in Morocco in 1578, most of his army was wiped out by vastly superior Arab forces. The king was reported killed in action (as was the sultan of Morocco and a deposed Arab prince) in the Battle of the Three Kings.

But for many Portuguese, Sebastian wasn't dead, only missing in action; his body was never found. He would return, they believed, and save the country from a power play by Spain. So enticing was the rumour, spread by alleged eye-witnesses and others, that a series of unconvincing impostors turned up claiming to be the missing king. It took years for the Portuguese to accept the reality. But in times of national despair they still, like young Sebastian, can't help dreaming. The syndrome is known as Sebastianism.

The Worst of Times

On All Saint's Day, November 1, 1755, the earth moved. The earthquake, centred off the Algarve coast, was the most terrible disaster of the age. It killed thousands as far away as Lisbon, inspiring Voltaire to write his great philosophical novel *Candide*. Closer to the epicentre, the Algarve's churches and castles were razed; fire from church candles spread to burn down houses; and a tidal wave completed the devastation. When the dead had been unearthed and reburied and the wounded tended to, the rebuilding began. In most towns, they collected the stones of the old church and put up a new one. Elsewhere, when you come across a roomy square or garden, it may have replaced a flattened residential neighbourhood.

Napoleon's Fiasco

Portugal's devotion to England ("the Oldest Alliance", dating back to the 14th century) was often tested, as when Sir Francis Drake irreverently sacked Henry the Navigator's old haunts at Cape St. Vincent in 1587. At the beginning of the 19th century the alliance blunted Napoleon's master plan for Europe. He put pressure on Lisbon to ban British ships, but the Portuguese refused all demands and in 1807 Napoleon lost his patience. He invaded, prompting the Portuguese royal family to flee to Brazil. To the rescue came Sir Arthur Wellesley, the future Duke of Wellington, who led a British liberation army. Battles flared all over Portugal, including the Algarve, where ragtag local defenders of Olhão overcame a French occupation force and then sent word of the victory

A nostalgic relic of the 18th-century Algarve: the faded palace at Estói.

to the king in Brazil. The messengers were two local fishermen who *rowed* across the Atlantic with the news. But Brazil was to declare its independence in 1822, and the costs of supporting Portugal's African colonies became oppressive. The once-golden empire was going broke. The monarchy was overthrown in 1910.

Century of Change

The new republic of Portugal had no easy ride. There were strikes, demonstrations, assassinations, attempted and successful coups, and a whirling dervish of changing governments. The dictator-ship of Dr. António de Oliveira Salazar, which endured from 1932 to 1968, assured stability and helped economic recovery but neglected other aspects of society. Salazar's successor was overthrown in a military coup in 1974—the "carnation revolu-tion", a bloodless celebration of freedom. In 1986 the new Portugal was admitted to the European Community, which underwrote many of the Al-garve's new projects, from high-ways to the renovation of the fishing fleet. Isolated on the very edge of Europe, the Algarve used to have nowhere else to look but overseas; now Europe beckons. 11

On the Scene

After a couple of days at the beach or on the golf links, even if sightseeing is not your first priority, you'll be ready to explore the extremely varied world of the Algarve. In part because of difficult roads, it's bigger than you think. We've divided the territory into three big strips: the windward coast, the leeward coast, and the unspoiled inland towns and villages.

WINDWARD COAST

Cape St. Vincent, Sagres, Lagos, Portimão, Albufeira, New Resorts

The coast westward from Faro feels less Mediterranean, more like the Atlantic Ocean; its authenticity grows the farther west you go, until Cape St. Vincent, where the Atlantic lets you know it's in charge. The stunted bushes have been bent by years of gales, with the low-slung houses dug in for self-defence. Yet on a cloudless day when the ocean is as calm as a pond, the "end of the world" seems more like the beginning.

Cape St. Vincent

Except for the sunsets, only a lighthouse-keeper could love the

Need a saddle for the donkey? An artisan at Alte can fit all sizes.

barren south-westernmost point in Europe. Five families of lighthouse guardians huddle together in a compound, once a monastery, at the base of the big red-topped beacon. So many tourists come here nowadays that they've had to close the light to the public; unless you're very convincing, you won't get to climb the spiral steps to the big bulbs that signal ships up to 60 miles offshore. Still, you can look straight down the cliffside onto the ocean and roam around the lighthouse complex. Just out of the wind you're likely to see one of the keepers' wives taking the sun, crocheting baby shoes and bedspreads. You might end up taking home an unlikely souvenir. 13

A Saint's Legend

The peninsula got its name (Cabo de São Vicente in Portuguese) from the 4th-century martyr-priest, St. Vincent. During the Islamic occupation of Iberia, the saint's body was hidden in the Algarve, but as the centuries went by nobody could remember exactly where. After the Christian Reconquest, the legend goes, searchers failed to find St. Vincent's relics—until a pair of very special ravens led them to the hiding place. Not only that. As the relics were being shipped to Lisbon, the loyal ravens flew along. St. Vincent is Lisbon's patron saint, and the seal of the city shows the ravens and a sailing ship.

Sagres

Another finger of land projecting from the small town of Sagres is the promontory where, tradition says, Prince Henry the Navigator established his School of Navigation. On Sagres Point, 60 m (200 feet) directly above the waves, few vestiges of the prince's days remain. Fortress walls were built in Henry's time, but the centuries and storms took their toll. Not much was left after Sir Francis Drake raided the fortress in 1587 and torched the library. Then came the earthquake of 1755, after which the fortress was sturdily rebuilt. Inside, a small white chapel has survived, and on the ground there's a vast sundial or something symbolic in the form of a mariner's compass. We can picture Prince Henry, standing at the circle of stones with his staff of scientists and sailors, leading a lesson in geography. Most of the history here is in the imagination. But the austere prince's achievements in sending mariners beyond sight of land, replacing fear and ignorance with courage and knowledge, are as real as today's stream of satellite-guided ships turning this busy corner of the Atlantic.

2 THE TWO BEST BRIDGES Elegant design distinguishes two modern suspension bridges in the Algarve. Spanning the estuary of the **Arade River**, the bridge at Portimão has relieved chronic traffic congestion in the town. The sparkling international bridge over the **River Guadiana,** 6 km or 4 miles north of Vila Real, relegates the ferryboat fleet to the realm of nostalgia.

Lagos

Phoenicians, Romans and Moors first developed Lagos, and parts of the ancient city walls, much restored, still stand guard. But a modern statue of Henry the Navigator, holding a sextant and gazing out at the harbour, recalls the port city's most memorable role in history. Prince Henry was Governor of the Algarve, and this was his capital. His palace, like many historic buildings, was lost in the 1755 earthquake. His caravels, designed and built in Lagos, sailed from here into the unknown. The funds that supported his School of Navigation came from his gubernatorial perks, including a percentage of the Algarve tunny fishing business. He is said to have declined his commission on the slave trade, which began here. The captives that his mariners brought back from Africa were put up for auction in a small arcade, marked "Mercado de Escravos" (slave market), on the north-east side of what is now Henry the Navigator Square.

Igreja de Santo António

Lagos is proud of several historic churches, but the interior of St. Anthony's Church all but explodes with 18th-century rococo art. On the gilt walls and altar, a convention of angels hold up columns and each other. You'd never know it from the exuberant decorations, but this was the church of the Lagos regiment of the Portuguese army. See the gravestone, in the floor of the chapel, of the regiment's Irish commander, Hugh Beaty.

Museu Regional

Everything you might want to know about Lagos, and more, is stockpiled in the museum next door to the church. The collection runs from archaeology to numismatism, via handicrafts, fishing nets, and African sculptures caricaturing Portuguese colonial officials. In an array of religious art you'll find 16th-century vestments worn at a mass said for King Sebastian just before his suicidal crusade to North Africa. A startling modern statue of Sebastian by João Cutileiro, in Gil Eanes Square, pictures him as a weird astronaut with a mop of hair covering a cartoon face.

Beaches

Lively Lagos is not a resort in itself, but nearby beaches have spurred developments. Praia da Luz, once a whaling station, now exploits its big, curving bay for water sports. Burgau and Salema are fishing villages now in the grip of the tourism imperative. East of Lagos, Meia Praia is a long and inviting sandy beach. Offshore may be the last resting place of one or more 16th-century Spanish galleons loaded with gold and trinkets from Mexico. Farther east, the spacious Alvor beach is a favourite with windsurfers. The historic town of Alvor has one "must" for serious sightseers: the 16th-century parish church, with an elaborately carved portico in the Manueline style.

Ponta da Piedade

Along the cliffs between Lagos and Luz stand some of the Algarve's most evocative rock formations. Sand-blasted by the sea, Ponta da Piedade ("Piety Point") is an ensemble of hallucinations, free-standing and attached. The scene is impressive from above, but the nicest way to inspect the cliff faces and grottoes is from the sea aboard one of the excursion boats.

Portimão

The ancient Romans thought highly of the town's location at the mouth of the Arade River and called it Portus Magnus. Portimão grew into a vital fishing port and, almost by accident, a centre of tourism. A few years ago the fishing fleet was exiled from the centre of town—where the loading and unloading of great trawlers used to provide a gripping spectacle—to a new harbour across the river. And the main quay now deals in pleasure craft and excursions. On the quayside, charcoal grills turn out some of the most delicious—and cheapest—giant sardines you'll ever savour. They're about three times the size of the little fish that come in tins.

Park Benches

Just opposite the municipal tourist office, Largo 1° de Dezembro is a small city park with a difference. Beneath the trees, the park benches are adorned with azulejos, illustrated blue and white tile squares, picturing crucial events in Portuguese history. The name of the park refers to the first of December of 1640, when Portugal regained its independence from Spain.

Praia da Rocha

The beach that launched a million postcards, Praia da Rocha is within walking distance of Portimão. The beauty of the beach, dotted with splendid free-standing rock formations, can't be disturbed, but the cliffsides behind it are burdened with the high-rise fervour of tourism ventures. The metropolis has spread ever farther inland. The beach is ample enough to handle the crowds, thanks to tons of sand added during dredging operations to upgrade Portimão's harbour.

Weird rock formations congregate just beyond famous Praia da Rocha.

Carvoeiro

Mushrooming tourist facilities rise in an amphitheatre behind the small beach of Carvoeiro, hemmed in by cliffs. Yet somehow the fishing boats pulled up on the sand make it seem as if nothing has changed since simpler days. The coast along here is riddled with caves and coves; excursions in small boats are the ideal way to absorb the atmosphere. Snorkellers have a field day.

Nossa Senhora da Rocha

On a powerful promontory projecting into the ocean between two beaches stands a simple fishermen's chapel dedicated to Nossa Senhora da Rocha, Our Lady of the Rock. The little white church with a pyramidal roof has stood here for centuries, the place where sailors and fishermen prayed before going to sea. How many centuries isn't known, but there are details in Romanesque or even earlier style. The nearby fishermen's village of Armação de Pêra has been overtaken by high-rise tourism, but the golden beach is still a winner.

Albufeira

The most popular resort in all Portugal, with nearly 90 hotels, tourist apartments and rooming 17

Old town of Albufeira: the Moors bequeathed the jumbled street plan.

houses, somehow keeps its sense of balance. The beaches may be swarming with sunbathers, but fishermen still go about their business; a little crowd, some in bikinis, greets every arriving boat to look over the catch. The cobbled streets of the old town are devoted to commerce, as they must have been in Moorish times; today the endless outdoor market deals in everything from puppies for pets to live chickens and ducks for the cooking pot. Albufeira thrived during the Middle Ages, thanks to lively commercial links with North African ports. Its natural defensive position kept the Moors entrenched long after most other Algarve towns had fallen to the Christian Reconquest. The change of management cut off Albufeira's main source of prosperity, and the town sank back into its role as a fishing village. Centuries later, the very mixed blessing of tourism awoke the sleeping beauty.

The Old Town

The traditional heart of Albufeira has become a gardened plaza, barred to traffic, where pedestrians only can tread the mosaic tiles. Many bars and restaurants, some unconventional, keep the area lively into the wee hours.

(Some of the establishments position multilingual touts near their doorways to drag in the cosmopolitan customers, but otherwise it's all low-key, as in the rest of Portugal.) Although the hills above the whitewashed heart of town have been infested with ever bigger hotels, life down below is still as relaxed and agreeable as ever. You'll soon find your way to the tunnel conveniently cut through the cliff down to the beach, framed by surreal rocks, and to the neighbouring fishermen's beach.

Olhos de Água

This beach, one the last of the cliff-bordered stretches before the coast, assumes the flat, undramatic mode of the leeward zone. Olhos de Água used to be an obscure little fishermen's hideaway. The sandy beach is a delight, but traffic jams and incessant construction signal the end of the age of innocence. A natural phenomenon here is an undersea fresh-water spring, visible and usable only at low tide. When the tide comes in, the pressure of the submerged spring is said to create tricky tidal patterns. Olhos de Água means "eyes of water", and the fishermen paint all-seeing eyes on the prows of their boats, as superstitious seamen have been doing for centuries to ward off danger.

New Resorts

Between Albufeira and the provincial capital, Faro, developers have transformed farmers' fields into internationally known resort complexes. There are no towns, almost no history, only the character that the sponsors and architects chose to impose on their estates. Most are designed for upmarket clients who are willing to pay whatever it costs for all comforts and conveniences, from golf to gambling. In some places a Portuguese motif has been installed, elsewhere a vague Mediterranean style. The resorts are so big that a car is essential for getting from the beach to the shops to the villa.

Vilamoura

The front door of the Vilamoura holiday complex opens onto the Algarve's biggest marina, haven for hundreds of yachts from the seven seas. You don't have to be a sailor to be inspired by the sight of so many dream-boats, fluttering flags and flapping sails. Water sports is one of the chief selling points, but the creators of what's called Europe's biggest private-sector tourist enterprise didn't stop there. Golf galore, tennis, horseback riding, fitness centres, restaurants of many kinds, and nightlife—they're all in the master plan. The holidaymakers can stay in high-rise 19 hotels or blocks of flats or suburban villa colonies, each designed with a particular theme. Except for the marina waterfront there is no defined centre of attraction; cryptic direction signs abound on the curving roads of the Vilamoura suburban sprawl, so you could easily drive around in circles just trying to get out.

History, Too

The promotors of Vilamoura weren't the first to see the virtues of the site. The ancient Romans built a harbour nearby and developed it as a fishing port, with a fish-salting industry, and cargo ships to export the fish to overseas markets.

Near the present marina, in the archaeological zone of Cêrro da Vila, excavations show the underpinnings of a Roman town, including a water system, walls and mosaics. A small museum here displays vestiges of Roman, Visigothic and Moorish development.

Quarteira

While Vilamoura is a custommade holiday megalopolis that was planned down to the last street light and lawn sprinkler, the next town eastward is a real fishing village that has been overwhelmed by mostly haphazard tourist development. Quarteira's success depends on its sprawling, golden sand beach. The fishermen's village remains, essentially unspoiled, but an outbreak of high-rise hotels and blocks of flats now looms over the traditional core. You are more likely to be offered "tea like mother used to make" than a *bica* of strong black Portuguese coffee. Still, Quarteira's weekly outdoor market is a treat for the tourists as well as an essential for the locals. You can buy a canary or a pigeon, fresh fruits and vegetables, homemade cheese and honey… or a plastic pail and a mop.

Two Last Resorts

Vale do Lobo means "valley of the wolf", but the only howls come from golfers who miss a putt. The fanciful name doesn't seem to deter holidaymakers in search of a planned resort community with first-class golf and tennis facilities.

Just to the east, Quinta do Lago is an even more luxurious affair, with tasteful villas discreetly dispersed in a superbly landscaped park setting. The promoters claim this is Europe's "lowest-density living area"—meaning, mainly, that money is no object. The resort's 36-hole golf course lives up to the stated standard of excellence. Quinta do Lago means farm by the lake; the lake in question is salt.

LEEWARD COAST

Faro, Olhão, Tavira, Monte Gordo, Vila Real de Santo António, Castro Marim, Alcoutim

From the Algarve's provincial capital, Faro, eastward to the Spanish border, the *Sotavento* or leeward coast provides a restful contrast to the challenging cliffs and coves of the windward zone. Here the mood becomes more Mediterranean. The Man Against the Sea challenge dissolves into the security of a sunbather's paradise, a succession of enormous children's beaches, sand dunes and lagoons. If it's all too relaxing, stimulate the mind with some sightseeing in the coast's historic towns, and up the Guadiana River.

Faro

The provincial capital feels provincial indeed—more like a bucolic backwater than a dynamic centre of tourism and commerce. Enhancing the impression is the sight of the low-rise old town with its whitewashed houses and palm trees. Other Algarve towns were built around noisy, smelly ports harbouring deep-sea trawlers, but Faro today has a sleepy, shallow pleasure port on its doorstep. Yet Faro has had its epochs of importance—under the Romans it coined its own money—and the traces of

grandeur are still there, along with a provincial charm and friendliness.

A Troubled History

Faro has been overrun, and often pillaged, by some of the most distinguished invaders in Europe and beyond. In AD 418 the Visigoths seized the town from the Romans. The Moors arrived from North Africa in AD 714 and made it the capital of a principality. The leader, Ben Said Ben Harun, is said to have given his name to the town, as Harun gradually evolved into Faro. (On the other hand, *farol* is the Portuguese word for beacon, an easier derivation to swallow.) Portugal's King Alfonso III reconquered Faro from the Muslims in 1249. No less a combatant than the Earl of Essex sacked the city in 1596 on behalf of Queen Elizabeth I. And in 1808 Napoleon's forces came this way. After all this deadly commotion, today's tourist invasion is something of a relief.

Around the Port

Since the tidal flat became silted up, ocean liners and show-off yachts have to avoid the inner

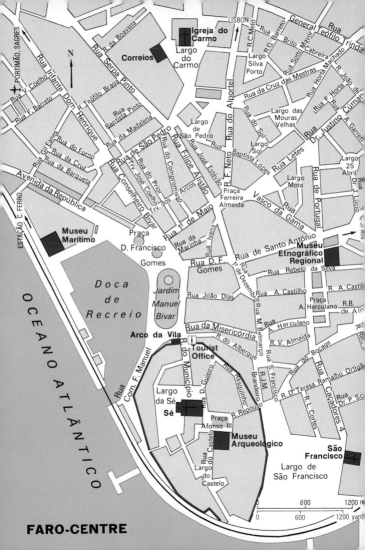

FARO-CENTRE

port of Faro. Only small craft can manoeuvre under the low railway bridge that provides the sole access. Despite these shortcomings the harbour is more attractive than ever. They've built an inviting waterfront promenade from which you can watch the little craft coming and going and, directly below you, big fish lazing around in full view. Just inland, the Jardim Manuel Bivar is a palm-shaded municipal garden with flowering trees, children's swings and slides, handicrafts stalls, artistically designed pavements and a popular indoor/outdoor café.

The Walled Town

The way into the old walled town is through the Arco da Vila, a fine 18th-century arch with a family of storks ensconced atop the bell tower. (The tourist office is just next door.) The worn cobbled streets lead to the Sé (cathedral), which has been through centuries of frightful change. The site is said to have been used first for a Roman temple, then a Visigothic church, then a mosque, before the Reconquest built a Romanesque-Gothic church in the middle of the 13th century. After each of the disasters that followed over the centuries, it was expanded and improved, but the steeple seems to have been chopped off; the truncated bell tower is topped by a crowing cock weathervane. Inside, a brilliantly decorated Baroque organ is a happy highspot, well endowed with trumpet-blowing angels and other joyous images.

Museu Arqueológico

The full name is the Prince Henry Archaeological and Lapidary Museum, and it occupies an old, whitewashed convent virtually next door to the cathedral. Among prehistoric and Roman artefacts dug up in Faro and its

---

CAUGHT IN THE MIDDLE

Why did England attack the Algarve in the late 16th century—Francis Drake sacking Sagres, the Earl of Essex setting fire to Faro? Whatever happened to the Anglo-Portuguese alliance of 1386? You can blame King Philip II of Spain, who invaded Portugal, proclaimed himself king, and thus dragged Portugal into Spain's war against England. The Faro incident was only a minor foray for Essex, who became a national hero in England when he captured the Spanish bastion of Cádiz. But court intrigues were the death of him. Five years after Faro and Cádiz, Queen Elizabeth had him beheaded for treason.

23

suburbs there are artistic statues and—star of the show—a 2,000-year-old Roman mosaic portrait of a wildly bearded Neptune. Part was lost before archaeologists got to the site in downtown Faro, but otherwise it's in mint condition.

More Museums

On the waterfront, sharing the building of the harbour master, the Museu Marítimo is full of old navigational instruments, ship models, maps, and displays devoted to the fishing industry. In the town centre, just beyond the pedestrians-only shopping zone, the Museu Etnográfico Regional tells the story of Algarve culture through typically furnished reassembled houses and examples of handicrafts. Traditional costumes for all occasions are displayed. Most of the handicrafts are still produced somewhere up in the hills—nowadays for the tourist market.

Igreja do Carmo

Opposite Faro's main post office, the Carmelite Church dates from the beginning of the 19th century. Its graceful towers and façade are rather hemmed in by the modern city, but the interior has some notable Baroque wood-carvings and paintings. If you're not queasy about it, have a look at the Capela dos Ossos (chapel of bones), reachable through a side entrance. The 19th-century vault was constructed from the skulls and bones of the monks and parishioners.

Faro's Beaches

Sand bars protecting Faro from the open ocean give the city its beaches, but you have to get there by car, bus or boat. Out past the airport, Ilha de Faro (Faro Island) is linked to the mainland by a bridge, so it tends to attract crowds of locals and tourists. If the tide on the ocean side is too strong, move your bathing to the

3 THE THREE BEST VILLAGES In the hills of the Algarve, far from the beach throngs, some villages are so unspoiled that they're on the tourist excursion itineraries. **Alte** is a model town with a view over a natural wooded landscape. Nearby **Salir** has the ruins of a castle and heartwarming panoramas. **Caldas de Monchique** is a very old-fashioned spa in a cool forest near the highest point of the Algarve.

lagoon side, where the water is usually calm. Only a boat can take you to neighbouring Ilha da Barreta, with plenty of sands. At the eastern end of the isle is a lighthouse and a small village.

Igreja de São Lourenço

Inland, a few miles west of Faro, a pleasant white country church stands on a hill overlooking the busy highway. Inside is a wonderful surprise. The Church of São Lourenço was built early in the 18th century when the villagers' prayers to St. Lawrence were answered: desperate for water, they suddenly found a gushing source. In gratitude, they decided to honour the saint with a very special kind of church. The inner walls and vaulted ceiling are all but completely covered in ensembles of azulejos, painted glazed tiles recounting the life of the saint. The only relief from the hypnotic effect of blue and white panels is the gilded altar. São Lourenço is one of the few Algarve churches spared by the 1755 earthquake.

Olhão

They call it the "cubist city", because of the architecture in the old town—boxy whitewashed houses with terraces instead of the red-tile roofs and decorative chimneys typical of the Algarve. Many of the houses have outside

---

HOORAY FOR SARDINES!

Sardines, rich in calcium and protein, are good for you. They are good, too, for the Algarve economy. In ports like Olhão, big-time canneries process the fish and export mountains of tinned sardines to the world. The name "sardine" comes from the Latin *sardina*, meaning a little fish suitable for pickling. But sardines—young herrings, really—come much bigger than the ones you uncover in the can. See and taste the difference at any oceanside restaurant in the Algarve.

---

stairways leading to lookout towers, ideal for checking up on fishermen husbands or anticipated pirate attack. The architectural style, and the town itself, developed long after the Moors had been tossed out of Portugal. The inspiration, though, was North African, brought here by Olhão boatmen who engaged in trade with Morocco in the 18th and 19th centuries.

'Noble Town'

Olhão emerged from almost total obscurity in 1808 to become the darling of Portuguese patriots. Under Napoleon's yoke, as the saying went, the Algarve in general was resigned to its fate as 25

an occupied territory. One day, when the French troops posted an edict on the door of the parish church, it was torn off. In the insurrection that followed, Olhão volunteers with the most primitive weapons captured the French garrison and proclaimed the restoration of independence. When the Portuguese king, exiled in Brazil, received the news—hand-carried across the Atlantic by daring local boatmen—he bestowed the title, "Noble Town of Olhão of the Restoration". The incident inspired Portuguese resistance elsewhere, and an epic poem entitled "The New Argonauts".

Fishermen's Wharf

Fishermen from Olhão go as far afield as Newfoundland to harvest the national fish, cod. Closer to home, they drag in tons of sardines, most of which are gobbled up by the local canning factory, and bigger fish and seafood to satisfy regional demand. As you'd expect in a fishermen's town, the local fish market is well worth a look. Next door, in an identical hangar-like building on the waterfront, is the everything-else market, with inviting displays of fruits, vegetables, meat and even hardware.

Small-time fishermen in shallow port of Faro, the provincial capital.

Offshore

The low-lying islands that protect Olhão's harbour are easily reached by ferries. Close to shore, the Ilha de Armona is only 15 or 20 minutes away from the bustle of the port. There are miles of beaches, and the swimming is comfortable in the sheltered sea. The Ilha da Culatra, more distant, mixes fishing villages and holiday beach huts. Neither island has cars. The barrier reef is the seaward boundary of the Ria Formosa Natural Park, extending from west of Faro nearly to the Spanish border. Conservationists and migrating birds love it.

Fuseta

In this small fishing port just east of Olhão, the men who aren't fishing are building boats or raking the blinding white crystals as the water in the salt pans evaporates under the sun. Fuseta's tourist development is on a small scale, but ferries from here go to the beachy reef—to Armona and the Ilha de Tavira.

Tavira

Fishermen and aristocrats have always coexisted in Tavira, a small city of great charm. The aristocrats built discreet mansions and distinguished churches, making this one of the most attractive of Algarve destinations. The fishermen bring colour 27 to the quayside and delicacies to the local restaurants. It's all unspoiled, and but for the parking problems you'd never know the age of tourism had overtaken the Algarve.

Tavira is said to have been founded by the Phoenicians or the Carthaginians. The Roman era is best represented by the seven-arch stone bridge spanning the River Gilão in the middle of town—much restored but still essentially the original design (pedestrians only).

'Algarvian Rome'
Tavira is a city of churches, well over a dozen, by the most conservative estimate. Some authorities put their number at three dozen, but more than a few are closed. Stretching things a bit, local promoters have come up with a snappy slogan: "the Algarvian Rome". The churches suffered in the earthquake of 1755. So did the castle, of which only the restored walls remain. From here you get an overall view of the city and its unusual pyramidal roofs.

Santa Maria do Castelo
The castle's own church, St. Mary of the Castle, dates from the 13th-century Christian Reconquest, when it was built on the ruins of a mosque. The great earthquake left little standing except the original Gothic portal. This is the church where King John I knighted his sons, including the future Henry the Navigator, after their conquest of the North African Muslim stronghold of Ceuta.

The 16th-century Church of the Misericórdia, just down the hill, is pronounced a splendid example of Renaissance art. Flanked by Saints Peter and Paul, the original portal is also given the seal of approval of the royal crown and the city's coat of arms.

Câmara Municipal
City Hall, where the main street runs into the triangular Praça da República, reflects the sobriety of Tavira. Medieval arches run the length of the imposing building, an arcade that's handy for avoiding the midday sun—or a shower. On the ground floor of the city hall you'll find the municipal tourist office, where brochures, maps and advice are dispensed. The latest brochure lists nine churches of interest.

Quayside
The atmospheric covered market on the Tavira waterfront, dated 1887, features shiny fruits and vegetables. Down the quay, fishermen repair their nets and exchange gossip between engagements. They have to finish work before low tide, when the

River Gilão leaves boats high and dry. Then birds flock over the riverbanks rich in shellfish to snap up supper.

Until the 1970s Tavira's fishermen used to take part in what was nicknamed the bull-fights of the sea, when highly organized killing squads ambushed and harpooned shoals of tuna just offshore. The fish have cleverly moved farther out to sea. As for the tourists, they head for Ilha de Tavira, on a giant sandbank protecting Tavira from the ocean. Buses from the centre of town connect with ferries to the island. A few kilometres farther east, Cabanas is little more than a handful of tourist apartments, restaurants and bars within walking distance—at low tide—of the sandbank sheltering the village.

Monte Gordo

The Algarve's easternmost coast turns into a whale of a beach—so big and perfect that holiday-makers from many countries keep coming back year after year. Behind Monte Gordo's fabulous fine-sand beach, unfortunately, rises a hodge-podge of overdevelopment, in which nondescript hotels and apartment blocks overshadow traditional houses. City planners everywhere ought to take note of the results of these excesses. The golden-sand beach is about 10 km (6 miles) long, so where the urbanization peters out there are pine trees and dunes in the background and room to escape the crowds. One of the attractions of Monte Gordo is its gambling-and-nightlife casino, right on the beach.

Vila Real

The full name is Vila Real de Santo António—the royal city of St. Anthony. It has a curious history and appearance. Now a busy fishing port, the city rose from nothing in five months of 1774 in a bid to impress the Spaniards across the Guadiana River, the frontier. The idea belonged to the Marquis of Pombal, the hard-driving administrator of King Joseph I. It

---

THE CAROB TREE

The big, wizened carob tree is strangely beautiful, and useful too. The fruit it produces, in very long, bean-like pods, is officially considered edible, but mostly by livestock. Processed, though, it is a useful, high-calorie additive to foods. Carob seeds are so much alike that they are supposed to have served as the first standard of goldsmiths and jewellers—the original carat.

was Pombal who rebuilt Lisbon after the earthquake, and Vila Real follows the same grid plan as the capital's Baixa district, minus the architectural elegance. The main square features black and white cobblestones laid in a sun-ray pattern emanating from an obelisk obsequiously dedicated to Pombal's patron, the king; orange trees border the plaza. Pombal had even grander plans for Vila Real, which he envisaged as a centre of trade, industry, fishing and administration. But luck ran out for the marquis—and the town—when the king died and a new regime swept him from power.

Escudos and Spanish pesetas are equally welcome here, with local merchants pushing whatever appeals to visitors from across the river. Now that a bridge links the two countries a few kilometres north of Vila Real, the ferry service is secondary. Either way, it's an easy excursion to the Andalusian town of Ayamonte.

Ayamonte

Spanish Ayamonte and Vila Real are as different as Spanish and Portuguese bullfights. In Portugal the bull leaves the ring alive. (In Ayamonte, where peeling bullfight posters add to the gaiety of the walls, the merchants would hate you to leave without buying something silly for a souvenir, like a miniature bull or a minuscule bullfighter's sword.) Ayamonte is bigger than Vila Real, with a more sophisticated business district in a pleasant pedestrian zone. The government-run *parador* high above the town provides the best vantage point for a strategic survey of the two countries, now European partners, and the slow-moving river that divides them.

Castro Marim

Before there was Spain, the defenders of Castro Marim glared across the Guadiana River at the possible dangers to the east. In Roman times the river marked the dividing line between the

4 THE FOUR BEST BEACHES The biggest of the best is **Monte Gordo,** where the ocean is calmer and warmer. Runners-up for sheer space and attractiveness: **Vilamoura/Quarteira,** the photogenic **Praia da Rocha,** and **Meia Praia,** near Lagos. Better yet, discover your own secret cove.

A non-regal back street in Pombal's ostentatious border town, Vila Real.

provinces of Lusitania and Baetica, the forerunners of Portugal and southern Spain. The Romans left a fortress, waterworks, a hospital, and a prison so dreadful it would dissuade most lawbreakers. After five centuries of Moorish occupation the Christian army restored Portuguese rule. In 1319 the Order of Christ (successors of the Knights Templar) made Castro Marim their headquarters; Henry the Navigator was a grand master. In the 17th century, when relations with Spain had deteriorated, the Portuguese built a second fort dominating the river. All's quiet on the eastern front these days, so most of the action is in the marshland below the fortifications, a nature reserve.

Alcoutim

Up the river from Vila Real—it makes a winning boat excursion—this port also faces the Spanish "threat": the Andalusian town of Sanlúcar de Guadiana. Alcoutim's ancient castle, on a hilltop, looks out on Sanlúcar's castle across the river. The red-roofed, whitewashed Alcoutim parish church has a Renaissance portal. Otherwise, there's not much to see except for the clear-running river and the shy inhabitants of a sleepy provincial town. 31

INLAND

Aljezur, Fóia, Monchique, Silves, Alte, Loulé,
São Brás de Alportel, Estói

For the great escape from the crush of tourism, take a car or bus inland from the beach. Within a few kilometres you're in another world, another age, where peasants tend their olive orchards and vineyards and gravitate to the simple village tavern for a glass of wine or an espresso. The farther inland you go the less populous the Algarve becomes. The motorway from the Spanish border, which rushes through truly unspoiled country, signposts many of the towns in our survey, but the fun comes on the back roads. This chapter, mixing rustic hamlets and historic hill towns, follows the map from west to east.

Aljezur

The name couldn't be more Arabic. Founded by the Moors, Aljezur was the last town in the Algarve to fall to the Christian Reconquest, in 1249. The story goes that the bastion would have held out even longer had it not been for a Moorish maiden who opened the gates to the Portuguese foe; one of the besieging knights had stolen her heart. The imposing ruins of the castle—what's left after the 1755 earth-quake—are still there on its hill-top, the highest of three in this curiously arranged town. There are two churches, the newer one up the hill from the old. A civic-minded bishop tried to move the the town to higher altitude to get away from a low-lying infestation of mosquitoes. He built the new church as a centre of attraction, but most of the townsfolk failed to follow. Aljezur is the gateway to some of the loveliest, wide open west-coast beaches, most notably Monte Clérigo and Arrifana.

Fóia

This is the summit of the Algarve, a modest claim in a province that rises from sea level to an altitude just over 900 m (nearly 3,000 feet). But Fóia is a cool escape from summer's heat at the beach, enhanced by the fragrance of mountain herbs and wild flowers. Actually, it's often so windy that you may decide to buy a sweater, sold on the spot by the merchants who meet the excursion coaches. That's all there is at Fóia—just the souvenir stalls, a bar, a restaurant and an obelisk marking the summit. On a clear day the view from here is

For every taste: hand-made pottery, and more, by the side of the road.

predictably sensational, reaching from the Sagres peninsula to the beaches of Portimão.

Monchique

The only road to Fóia starts lower down the mountain in the small, hilly market town of Monchique, which also enjoys panoramas of the countryside. The white-washed parish church is distinguished by a Manueline portal decorated with carved knots that were supposed to evoke the sea during the age of exploration. Above the town are the ruins of a 17th-century Franciscan monastery, abandoned after the earthquake a century later. The people

of the Serra de Monchique, the hills of Monchique, produce some admired handicrafts and a much-prized ham. The hills, which provide the Algarve's protection from cold northern winds, get enough rainfall to encourage the most varied vegetation— eucalyptus, arbutus, pine, oak, and roadside flowers as cheering as mimosa and rhododendron.

Caldas de Monchique

The big hotels along the coast have fitness centres and all the trimmings, but the original health resort of the Algarve is Caldas de Monchique, a spa the Romans first developed. At the end of the 33

THE CORK CROP

Does it hurt the cork oak tree to have its bark removed every 10 years or so? We have no definitive answer, but the poor thing looks as bereft as a newly shorn sheep. Portugal is Europe's leading cork producer, so the bottle of French Champagne you pop may well have been corked with the processed harvest of that desolately naked Algarve tree. Local craftsmen also turn odd lots of cork into cute souvenirs.

15th century King John II came here to take the waters; unfortunately he died of various excesses very soon thereafter. This leafy backwater south of Monchique has lost most of its glamour since it flourished in Edwardian times. But there's a certain charm, and the least you can do is sample the health-giving if smelly water as it emerges piping hot from the source. It's free. Caldas de Monchique water is bottled here and served, cold, in bars and restaurants all over the province.

Silves

Rising above a lazy river in a zone of citrus orchards and weeping willows, Silves was once a Moorish capital of gardens, palaces and culture. Much fought over and much restored, the old red citadel surmounting the town is a solid reminder of a vanished era of greatness. It all began with the Phoenicians, and then the Romans, who may have been the first to build a castle. At the time, the river was a serious waterway, a main highway of Iberian commerce. Now the Arade is so silted at Silves that anything bigger than a rowing boat is liable to run aground.

Moorish Xelb

Arab invaders from Yemen occupied Silves in AD 711, and it remained under Islamic rule for the better part of five centuries. It was known, and widely admired, as Xelb, the capital of the Algarve. In the best of times, the 12th century, under cultured Almohad rule, the city was praised for its beautiful buildings and abundant markets, and the pure Arabic spoken by the residents. "They are verse-makers, eloquent and well-spoken," added a noted Arab geographer. (He also pronounced the locally grown figs divine.) The reconquest of Silves from the Muslims was a long, disastrous series of sieges. Crusaders seized and pillaged the city in 1189 but the Moors regained control in 1191. Finally, in the middle of the 13th century the Arabs were definitively dislodged. But by then the town was a shambles.

Silves Castle

The centuries-old crenellated walls of the castle contain embrasures for archers. The Great Tower faces north, for that was the route attackers customarily chose. You can wander along the perimeter walls and imagine the battles and sieges while looking out onto the farms and the town. Inside the battlements all is peaceful. Trees and flowers relieve the military atmosphere; a beer festival takes place here every summer. A bronze statue of Sancho I, fiercely holding a deadly looking sword, honours the king who temporarily liberated Silves in 1189. A huge well, called the Dogs' Cistern (*Cisterna dos Cães*), supplied the castle's defenders with water, but it was thirst that forced the Muslim troops to surrender to Dom Sancho.

Silves Cathedral

Like much else in Silves, the cathedral, founded in the 13th century, has its story of disappointment. It hasn't had a bishop in residence since 1579 when the town was eclipsed by Faro. Also, the remains of King John II, who died after some over-indulgences at nearby Monchique, were moved to a more regal location a few years later. And then there was the 1755 earthquake, which finished off earlier quake damage. The cathedral, Gothic in the beginning but tending to the baroque over centuries of repairs and improvements, somehow retains its early dignity. It is preserved as a national monument.

Museu de Arqueologia

In 1990 a new Municipal Museum of Archaeology was opened in a very old mansion in Rua das Portas de Loulé, near the town barbican. The captions

HOMESICKNESS REMEDY

This Arabian Nights story is supposed to have happened in many places, from Persia to Turkey to Spain. But the Algarve, and specifically Silves, claims the legend as its own. Once upon a time, an Arab potentate took a Nordic princess as his wife. She pined for the snows of home, and ultimately fell into a coma. Distraught, the king ordered all the fields surrounding his castle planted with almond trees. As spring arrived, the sight of a sea of white almond blossom revived her. To this day the view lifts the spirits.

National monument: the cathedral of Silves, begun in the 13th century.

are in Portuguese only, but the exhibits—from Stone Age axe-heads to medieval pottery—are well chosen and displayed. Some ceramics from the Moorish era are more beautiful, and colourful, than almost any available today. The single most gripping exhibit is a nicely renovated ancient cistern with a spiral staircase descending around its circumference. Archaeological discoveries were dredged up from its mysterious depths.

Cruz de Portugal

On the road out of Silves toward São Bartolomeu de Messines you pass the Cross of Portugal, a

monument to the Reconquest, which may date from the 16th century. It is beautifully carved from a single piece of limestone, with Christ crucified on one side and descended on the reverse. Protected by a modern pyramidal roof, the monument is at the centre of a small garden. Nobody knows who the sculptor was, or where it comes from (the type of stone is foreign to southern Portugal).

Alte

Once proclaimed the Algarve's most typical village, Alte is so quaint that the locals hang about waiting for tourists to gawk at.

They take the sun or the shade depending on the season and time of day, and puff on their pipes as if hoping to be immortalized in a photo.

Fans of history and art won't want to miss the parish church, with a Manueline portal and other 16th-century features on the inside. The whitewashed houses of the village all have original touches, architectural, decorative or floral, and the chimneys are charming.

On the edge of town, a refreshing brook burbles through a tree-shaded park on its way to irrigate the citrus, fig and pomegranate trees in the fertile valley below. The views of the landscape from Alte are as fetching as any in the region.

Salir

Another attractive hill village, Salir, has a 16th-century parish church and, more unusual, the remains of a Moorish castle above the town. Archaeologists are intrigued, for this is one of the few strictly Arab vestiges in the Algarve. The castle is in a desperately dilapidated state, but don't despair—the views over the countryside from the heights of Salir are an inspiration. At the village's Sunday market you can buy a hand-made wooden ladder, or any imaginable farm implement.

Loulé

This dynamic regional centre, with a big, modern shopping zone, parking meters and all, was elevated to the rank of a city as recently as 1988. Yet a small-town pace persists: there's always time for a coffee and a home-made pastry, or a shoe-shine *al fresco*—the shine of your life, by an expert. Lottery salesmen inoffensively hawk their tickets wherever unhurried people congregate. The obvious pole of attraction in this market town is the market itself—a strange building inspired by Moorish themes. The fruit and vegetable department, the display of fish, and the handicrafts all merit inspection. Doom-watchers report that the local artisans are dying out or gone to make money at the resorts, that you can hardly find a saddle-maker or brass-worker here any more.

Castle Area

Loulé's history is a bit vaguer than most. The Romans are thought to have been around, but the oldest monuments are the remains of a castle-cum-city-wall, built during the long Moorish occupation. They've restored parts of Loulé Castle, which is no competition for Silves but does add to the atmosphere. The battlements slice 37 through the centre of town, so you can climb one of the towers and look down on the crowded, complex layout of streets, another reminder of Arab times. Sharing a building with the tourist office, the municipal museum has a display of local handicrafts, a restored traditional kitchen, farm utensils, musical instruments, and archaeological bits and pieces.

Festivals

Loulé is the folklore capital of the Algarve. The festivals here are so colourful that Algarvians and tourists come from all over to watch. At Carnival time, flower-decked floats roll through the streets and participants affect far-out costumes. You are hardly likely to confuse Loulé with Carnival in Rio or Trinidad, but it's surely lots of fun. On Easter Sunday a mostly solemn procession carries a canopy-covered image of Nossa Senhora da Piedade, the town's patron saint, down from a 16th-century hilltop shrine. A bigger festival, a couple of weeks later, is not for the faint-hearted. This one reverses the direction: the celebrants run all the way up the hill.

Overshadowing the hilltop shrine of Mãe Soberana (the Sovereign Mother) is the hulk of a modern concrete cathedral, forever unfinished.

São Brás de Alportel

The people who live in São Brás are nicknamed *cachamorreiros*—meaning cudgel-wielders. They're proud of the epithet, too. It relates to an incident in 1596, when the British were rampaging through the Algarve, which was under Spanish control. As the invaders marched on São Brás, the locals got out their sticks and clubs and scared away the well-armed aggressors with their war cries. Echoes of the battle influence the São Brás celebration of Easter. Local men shouting *Aleluia!* march through town brandishing candles and home-made bouquets in honour of "the day of Christ's victory." São Brás prospered throughout the 20th century and now, incongruously, there are high-rise apartment blocks in the new part of town. The São Brás museum, the Museu Etnográfico do Trajo Algarvio, is devoted to the region's costumes through the ages.

Estói

About halfway between São Brás and Faro, the village of Estói has a sober parish church and an 18th-century palace with haunting, faded charm. The pink palace of Estói surmounts a brilliantly landscaped hill site, descending to a fish pool with goldfish in abundance and a garden below.

They're hooked on crocheting. The gossip helps pass the time, as well.

The palace is closed for a long-awaited renovation, but meanwhile the decorations visible from the garden are worth perusing—*azulejos* of sumptuous nudes and portraits of distinguished men, but mostly nudes.

Milreu

Archaeologists have been sifting through the Roman ruins of Milreu, within walking distance of Estói, for years.

The best discoveries—statues, pottery, jewels and mosaics—are found in museums in Faro, Lagos and Lisbon. (Before the archaeologists arrived on the spot, looters are thought to have snatched for themselves the most portable relics.)

The archaeologists first assumed that Milreu was a city, Ossonoba itself. Now they have decided that the capital, Faro, rates that honour. It seems that Milreu was the country villa of a Roman aristocrat, with facilities for his employees as well. There is a well-preserved sunken bath with mosaics of fish. Above ground are the ruins of a Visigothic basilica which had originally been a pagan temple dedicated to water gods. Intriguingly, it remained a pagan shrine long after Christianity had taken hold throughout the region.

39

EXCURSIONS

Once you're in the Algarve you're within striking distance of two fascinating, utterly different cities. Excursion firms run day-trips northward to Lisbon, the understated Portuguese capital, and eastward to the flamboyant Spanish city of Seville. Each city is about a four-hour coach trip from Faro, making a long day's outing. Obviously, a day-trip can only scratch the surface; you may well want to go back for more.

Lisbon

With its jolting trams, hilly cobbled streets and smoky bars, Lisbon is as quaint as the laundry hanging out to dry from its flowered balconies. The capital also offers magnificent views and striking historic monuments, and all the facilities of a contemporary city—from post-modern shopping to a Metro system pierced beneath the traffic jams.

On the trip from the Algarve, after hours traversing the grain fields and cork plantations of the Alentejo region, you enter Lisbon by crossing the Ponte 25 de Abril. This 1960s suspension bridge was, at the time, the longest in Europe. It was also named for the dictator, Salazar, an honour withdrawn after the 1974 revolution. Facing the city on the river bank high above the bridge's toll booths, the Statue of Christ the King is a smaller version of Rio de Janeiro's mountaintop Christ the Redeemer. Here the broad river—the Tagus (*Tejo* in Portuguese)—is on the last leg of its journey from mountainous eastern Spain to the Atlantic.

Discoveries

When the great Portuguese explorers left Lisbon on the way to their destinies, one of their last memories would be the sight of the Torre de Belém (Tower of Belém). Belém, which means Bethlehem, is the name of this historic part of the port. The elegant little riverside fortress, built early in the 16th century, is Portugal's most photographed landmark, a wonder of stone-carving.

Projecting over the river not far upstream is the modern Padrão dos Descobrimentos (Monument of the Discoveries), with a sculptural ensemble dominated by a statue of Henry the Navigator leading the way, hold-

Henry the Navigator presides over Tagus River, bridge in background.

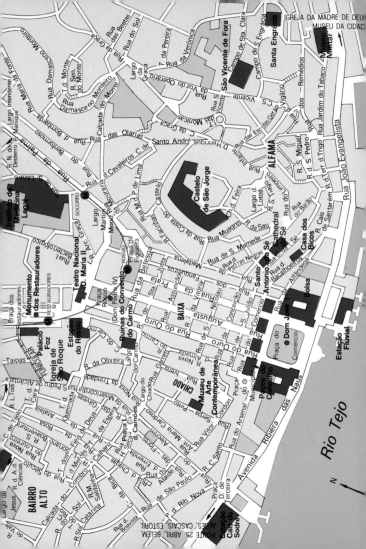

ing a model of a caravel. Near the base of the monument a map of the world inlaid in the pavement notes the dates and remarkable extent of Portugal's discoveries and overseas settlements.

Mosteiro dos Jerónimos

Lisbon's most formidable monument, the sprawling Jerónimos Monastery, is a triumph of the Manueline style of architecture, celebrating the early discoveries with intricate decorations evocative of the sea and faraway places. Like the Tower of Belém, it is classified as a World Heritage Site by UNESCO. Among the kings and heroes buried in the monastery's spacious church are the explorer Vasco da Gama and the national poet, Luis de Camões. On the west side of the complex are two worthy museums—the National Archaeological Museum and the Naval Museum.

The Baixa

About 6 km (4 miles) upstream from Belém, the river meets the heart of the city at Praça do Comércio (Commerce Square). Now one big parking lot, the plaza is surrounded on three sides by a graceful ensemble of arcades; the fourth side is open to the port. Through a triumphal arch you enter the Baixa (lowland) district, a grid of shopping streets lined with buildings of uniform height. When this part of town was wiped out by the quake of 1755, the bold reconstruction plan was decreed by the Marquis of Pombal, who put Lisbon back on its feet. The earthquake-proof Baixa leads to Lisbon's main square, the Rossio, once the venue for witch-burnings and bullfights. Now it's the ever-busy terminus for buses and taxis, home of outdoor cafés, flower stalls, and lively comings and goings.

Bairro Alto

From the Baixa a free-standing lift, a marvel of the Victorian era, goes up to the Bairro Alto, the "high neighbourhood". The Bairro Alto is noted for its nightlife, as earthy or sophisticated as you like. The Elevador de Santa Justa, inaugurated in 1902, was steam-operated until electric power was perfected. Tour guides usually attribute the construction to Gustave Eiffel, of Tower fame, but it isn't really so. The trip up or down is a treat.

Igreja do Carmo

Near the top exit of the lift, the 14th-century Carmelite Church is the ultimate monument to the great Lisbon earthquake. On All Saints' Day in 1755, when the church was crammed with worshippers, the tremor hit. The 43 roof fell in, and that's the way it stands today, Gothic arches open to the sky in a touching memorial to the victims. A small archaeological museum on the premises features some ancient mummies.

Castelo de São Jorge

From the Bairro Alto you look across all of central Lisbon to St. George's Castle, occupying the city's highest hill. The occupying Moorish forces erected the first major citadel on this spot, though the Romans had been there first. After the Christian Reconquest in the 12th century it was rebuilt and expanded into a royal palace. Much renovated since then, Lisbon's castle still shows the outline of its medieval muscles, and great views over the city. It also encloses a pleasant park inhabited by ravens, flamingos, pheasants, peacocks and other exhibitionist birds.

Cathedral

Lisbon's hillside cathedral (Sé) is embraced by the city; trams clang past the front door, and taxi brakes squeal. Its fortified façade indicates the dangers that surrounded the church in the 12th century, when it was begun. Earthquakes battered the building in the 14th, 16th and 18th centuries, giving generations of architects the chance to add innovations to its Romanesque and Gothic beginnings. The sacristy's museum of religious art includes a casket of relics of St. Vincent, the city's official patron saint.

St. Anthony of Padua, Lisbon's favourite saint, was born just down the street from the cathedral in 1195. His birthplace is now marked by the church of Santo António da Sé.

Alfama

The medieval street plan—or lack of a plan—of the hilly Alfama district adds to its peerless charm. You are bound to get lost, but the sights and sounds along the way are well worth the trouble. Some streets are so steep

---

IMPERIAL ECHOES

When the Portuguese empire finally self-destructed in the 1970s, hundreds of thousands of colonists hastily returned to Portugal. Somehow the mother country's less-than-glowing economy absorbed the tide of penniless refugee *retornados*. Many natives of troubled lands like Mozambique and Angola also fled to Lisbon. Thanks to easy-going racial relations, they, too, have done well. Clusters of Africans congregate in and around the Rossio, enlivening the exotic scene.

they are stepped, others so narrow you have to walk single-file, and others barely merit the title of alley. Decaying mansions with artistic decorations and dilapidated tenement houses singing with life line the streets and little squares. In among all the jumble there are churches, markets, bars and restaurants. And, everywhere, the spirited drama of daily neighbourhood life.

Gulbenkian Museum

Armenian-born billionaire Calouste Gulbenkian, who died in Lisbon in 1955, endowed this splendid museum, one of many cultural bequests to his adopted country. On show in this agreeable modern gallery are some of the thousands of works Gulbenkian acquired for his private collection, ranging from ancient Egyptian statues to Art Nouveau. The museum is first-rate in many departments, from Islamic art to Chinese porcelain to Europe's great masters—including Rembrandt, Rubens, Turner and Guardi. On the far side of a sculpture garden, the Gulbenkian Museum of Modern Art presents the definitive survey of 20th-century Portuguese art.

Museu de Arte Antiga

Recently restored to world standards, the National Museum of Ancient Art has three sensational star attractions. First, six large panels painted by the 15th-century Portuguese master Nuno Gonçalves portray contemporary figures like Henry the Navigator and King Alfonso V, along with clerics, businessmen and fishermen. It's a remarkable portrait of a cross-section of Portugese society as it looked at the time of the great discoveries. The Hieronymous Bosch triptych, *Temptations of St. Anthony,* is a mad, surrealistic experience, dated around 1500. Finally, Japanese screens painted in the 16th century record the astonishment of the islanders at the arrival of Portuguese missionaries and traders. The Japanese had never seen Persian horses, priests, buttons, or big European noses.

The Aqueduct

One final, startling sight you may come across in Lisbon. At first glance it might appear to be a Roman aqueduct in the middle of the city. In reality the Aqueduto das Águas Livres is an 18th-century enterprise, a 19-km (11-mile) water supply system that still serves Lisbon. Amazingly, too, construction of the aqueduct was finished in 1748, just seven years before the fateful earthquake knocked down everything in sight—except the aqueduct, which was unscathed.

45

Seville

Like Lisbon, Seville claims that its roots go back to mythical times. The Romans were here, and the Moorish occupation endured for five agitated centuries. Like Lisbon, Seville is a river port from which audacious expeditions of exploration were launched. Despite these background similarities, Lisbon and Seville are as different as a melancholy *fado* and a foot-stamping flamenco. For Seville is the most Spanish of all the cities of Spain, as flashy and fervent as Lisbon is unassuming.

La Catedral

The biggest cathedral in Spain stands on the site of the Great Mosque of Moorish Seville.

SING A SONG OF SEVILLE

Rossini's *Barber of Seville* gave the city a certain notoriety, but it wasn't the first time grand opera publicized Seville. Mozart's *Marriage of Figaro* and *Don Giovanni* contain Seville angles. Topping them all for local colour is Bizet's *Carmen,* starring a gypsy sexpot working in the cigar factory. (The enormous 18th-century building still exists, but now it houses the University of Seville.)

Begun in the 15th century in Gothic style, the construction effort, often interrupted, went on for four centuries. The main altar, with fabulous sculptural details, is protected by an 18th-century screen. The Capilla Real (royal chapel) features the tombs of King Alfonso X and his mother, Beatrice of Swabia. Elsewhere in the five-naved church stands an ostentatious tomb reputed to contain the well-travelled remains of Christopher Columbus (who had many Seville connections).

Among the hundreds of paintings in the chapels of the cathedral are works by Murillo, Zurbarán and Goya.

La Giralda

Seville's most visible and unforgettable landmark, rising alongside the cathedral, used to be a minaret. In the highly-cultured Almohad era of Islamic dominance, it was considered one of the three most beautiful minarets in the world (the others are in Rabat and Marrakesh, Morocco). The Reconquest spared it and converted it into a church bell tower.

You can climb up to the lookout level and take in the aerial views of the cathedral's buttresses and the city beyond. After eight centuries the exquisite Giralda, just under 100 m (320 ft)

Arabesques: sample of the sumptous details of Seville's Alcazar palace.

high, is still the tallest building in Seville.

Torre del Oro
Seville's other landmark tower is right along the Guadalquivir river bank. A squat but well-proportioned 12-sided tower, the Torre del Oro (Golden Tower) served the Moorish regime as a watch-tower. A chain from here to a tower on the opposite bank guarded the city from seafaring invaders. In the Golden Age of Spanish colonialism the tower was a warehouse for shipments of gold and silver from the New World. Now it houses a small maritime museum.

Archivo General de Indias
In the 16th century this harmonious Renaissance building served as the Commercial Exchange, where Seville's merchants negotiated the development of the booming new Spanish empire. Today it contains the Archive of the Indies, some 90 million documents recording every detail of the evolution of the New World—from the most mundane invoices filed by colonial bureaucrats to personal letters by Columbus and those who followed him. The architect, Juan de Herrera, also built the palace of El Escorial, near Madrid.

47

Alcázar Real

A palace here has housed Seville's rulers since the time of the ancient Romans. In spite of the Arabian Nights decor of the present Royal Palace, little is left from the Moorish era; almost all of the extravaganza of the Alcázar was built after the Reconquest, the work of Muslim artisans under the direction of the newly triumphant Spanish authorities. Filigree, arches and double marble columns give a special grace to the Patio de las Doncellas (Courtyard of the Ladies-in-Waiting). Intricate details and colour schemes enliven the dignity of the Salón de Embajadores (Ambassadors' Hall).

Barrio de Santa Cruz

The most picturesque neighbourhood in Seville, the Santa Cruz Quarter, is a whitewashed warren of Andalusian exotica. Before the Inquisition this was the old Jewish quarter, and one of the local churches—Santa María la Blanca—was originally a synagogue; its greatest work of art is a *Last Supper* by Murillo. The artist's studio has been re-created in Calle Santa Teresa. The Santa Cruz Quarter rewards the wanderer with pleasant surprises—flowered balconies and patios, artisan's workshops, blue-collar houses, mansions, and little plazas shaded by orange trees.

La Cartuja

The site of Seville's 1992 World's Fair, the island has been turned into a theme park and science-and-industry campus. La Cartuja is named after a Carthusian monastery founded there in 1400. Christopher Colombus often stayed with the monks, and he was buried there for a time.

Plaza de España

Expo-92 wasn't the city's first experience with a world's fair. In 1929 Seville hosted the Great Iberoamerican Exhibition, and it wasn't until 1988 that the deficit was finally paid off. One of the legacies of the 1929 fair is Plaza de España, a gigantic impression of a Spanish square—a semicircle, actually, with a canal round its inner rim. Ducks and rowing boats share the canal.

Museo Arqueológico

A fake Renaissance palace houses Seville's Archaeological Museum, an outstanding collection of Andalusian relics from the Stone Age to the Moorish era. From the ancient Roman city of Itálica, just north of Seville, the birthplace of Emperors Trajan and Hadrian, come giant statues. A mysterious earlier civilization produced the Carombolo Treasure, including gorgeous gold jewellery and the small statue of a long-haired goddess.

CULTURAL NOTES

Azulejos. Glazed, decorative tiles, most often blue and white. The art and technology came from North Africa during the Moorish occupation. Muslim artists were restricted to calligraphic and abstract designs, but the Portuguese developed illustrations of mythology, historical events and everyday life, evolving to religious and even satirical compositions. Illustrated *azulejos* are used to decorate anything from a café to a church. The Algarve's most splendid array of *azulejos* fills the walls and ceiling of the São Lourenço church near Faro.

Bacalhau. There's no accounting for tastes, certainly not for the Portuguese love affair with cod. They've been eating it with a passion since the first Portuguese explorers reached Newfoundland in 1501. Local seas are full of eminently edible fresh fish but the big attraction is *bacalhau*, dried and salted and tough as nails when it arrives from the other side of the Atlantic. With hundreds of recipes, the mystical cod can be dressed up to fulfil any Portuguese gourmet's dreams.

Bullfighting. Unlike the Spanish bullfight, the goal of the Portuguese *tourada* is not to kill the bull, just to dominate him while showing off some amazingly agile footwork. Bullfights in the old Portuguese style involve specialists dressed in 18th-century costumes mounted on exquisitely trained horses. When the prancing and dart-throwing are over, bullfighters afoot have to subdue the bull with their bare hands. Traditional bullfights start at 5 p.m. but in the Algarve, to escape the summer heat, the lights go on at 10 p.m.

Camões. In the age of Cervantes and Shakespeare, the national poet of Portugal, Luís Vaz de Camões, set his nation's literary standards for the centuries. His most dazzling work, the epic poem *Os Lusíadas*, links Greek mythology with the exploits of the Portuguese explorers. Camões (Camoens in English) knew faraway places first-hand—he served in Ceuta, Goa and Macau. He died on the verge of poverty in 1580.

Chimneys. Since Moorish times the Algarve skyline has been beautified by delicately filigreed chimneys. House-proud Algarvians commission latticed chimneys, generally white, in many fanciful forms—like mini-minarets or mushrooms. In olden days they were carved from tree trunks but ceramic or even cement is the modern medium.

Festivals. Local festivals, which normally honour a village's patron saint, combine religious fervour with gaiety: solemn processions of ecclesiastical and municipal dignitaries, followed by dancing and fireworks. The liveliest of all the Algarve *festas* occur in the hill town of Loulé, which also puts on a regionally famous Carnival.

Language. Close to 200 million people speak Portuguese, most of them in former possessions like Brazil and Angola. The language in Brazil has its own eccentricities in spelling and pronunciation, but they pose no problem for the millions of Portuguese addicted to the melodramatic Brazilian soap operas on television. A Romance language (the same family as Spanish and French), Portuguese has absorbed many words from Arabic.

Manueline. The Manueline style of architecture is named after King Manuel I, who presided over the golden age of Portuguese discoveries. Developed from late Gothic, Manueline details suggest the wonders of exploration—with stone-carvings of globes, sails, anchors, even exotic fruits embellishing church doors and columns. In the Algarve you can see Manueline details in churches of Monchique, Silves, Alvor, Lagos and Luz de Tavira.

Music. The Portuguese have been serious about music ever since Domenico Scarlatti worked as the court composer for King John V. The Algarve Music Festival, every spring, stages classical concerts in historic churches. The folk music of the Algarve cheerily accompanies square dances and jigs. In resort discos you'll hear Portuguese rock as well as international hits. Finally, don't miss an evening of *fado*, the songs that go straight to the Portuguese heart—mostly melancholy but not always so.

Saudade. Yearning, regret, nostalgia—an untranslatable Portuguese psychological condition leading to sentimental fatalism. It's what makes the *fado* so powerful.

Vinho. Most wines produced in the Algarve are red, full-bodied and very powerful. The biggest and best-known winery is at Lagoa, but there are also co-operatives at Lagos, Tavira and Portimão. The Algarve's after-dinner speciality is *medronho*, distilled from the strawberry-like fruit of the arbutus tree.

If you widen your horizons to Portugal in general, the choice of wines is overpowering—red, white, rosé, and even "green". *Vinho verde* is a young semi-sparkling white wine that goes well with seafood.

Shopping

The easy way to begin your shopping spree is to survey the souvenir shops in the resorts. Armed with an idea of the range of goods on sale and the maximum prices, you can move closer to the source at the roadside shops and weekly markets. Finally, you may come upon artisans at work in the hill villages. Even if the prices are no bargains, the memories can't be beaten.

What to Buy

The most practical purchase you can make in the Algarve must be knitwear, especially the rugged, hand-made pullovers of the sort that sailors and fishermen wear. It all happens in the hill country where the sheep are sheared, the wool is washed, combed and spun, and then the knitting needles begin to click.

Cleverly, they're often sold where it's windy—at end-of-the-world Sagres and top-of-the-world Fóia.

The most impractical purchase? You might suddenly crave a saddle and harness for your donkey, or a wrought-iron gateway for your garden.

Whether you use it for decorating your kitchen or actually cooking in it, a *cataplana* is one of the most typical items you can buy. Algarve artisans still turn

out these hinged woks, elementary pressure-cookers, and the top-of-the-line models are handsome.

More for the kitchen: ceramic bowls, plates, pitchers and cups, and they come in gaily coloured hand-painted sets. The Algarve also produces tons of rough pottery, such as garden pots and amphorae, and the pots that local fishermen use as octopus traps. You can take home an elegant Algarve chimney—or a miniature version no bigger than a pepper-shaker. Perhaps brighten up your mantelpiece, kitchen or patio with *azulejos*—a single painted square or a whole illustrated ensemble. They will do you a wall according to your own specifications.

In some fishing ports, once the nets are mended the women traditionally turn to more delicate 51 needlework: embroidery or lace. You'll often see them working in the doorway of their home, or more congenially in groups in some corner shaded from the sun. In the shops you'll find everything from bedspreads to table napkins. The best needlework in all Portugal, from the island of Madeira, is also sold in the Algarve.

Also imported—from the Alentejo, the buffer province between the Algarve and Lisbon—are beautiful hand-made rugs, noted for their happy designs and colours. The Algarve produces patchwork quilts, which include strips of hand-woven linen.

Brassware and copperware have been an Algarve speciality since Moorish times. Look for delicately executed trays, candlesticks, and pots and pans.

Gold and silver filigree, originally a Moorish art form, turns up in intricately fabricated model caravels and roosters and fantasy jewellery.

Wickerwork comes in many varieties and sizes—mats, hats, bags, carpets, even furniture.

Woodwork has always been a local speciality—from elaborate donkey carts to furniture to figurines. Treasure chests, too.

After they've made millions of corks for wine bottles, the odds and ends from the cork harvest end up in the hands of artisans, who carve miniature sculptures, placemats and assorted knick-knacks.

For an easily portable, inexpensive souvenir of Portugal, pick up a disc or cassette of cheerful Algarve music, or the soulful melodies of the national lament, the *fado*.

Finally, an easy choice for a gift or souvenir: take home a bottle of Portuguese wine—a fine port or Madeira, or a bottle of local spirits: *medronho*, distilled from the arbutus berry, *amêndoa amarga*, an almond liqueur, *brandymel*, a honey-flavoured brandy.

5 THE FIVE BEST BUYS Algarve artisans, mostly hidden in the countryside, produce useful and attractive souvenirs. Look for hand-made **knitwear** (rugged sweaters), **embroidery** (more subtle needlework), **brassware** (candlesticks and trays), **pottery** (hand-painted bowls), and **wickerwork** (everything from baskets to furniture).

Dining Out

Nobody's showing off in an Algarve restaurant, unless it's the baby clams in the display cabinet launching jets of water into the air, or the lobsters clawing to prominence in their tank. The waiters are down-to-earth and helpful. The chef is too busy in the kitchen to make a fuss. The food he's cooking is wholesome and abundant, not pretentious. You'll like it.

Start Here

For the Portuguese, breakfast is inconsequential—coffee with toast or rolls, butter and jam. Incidentally, the delicious bread, which always looks and tastes home-made, recalls an earlier, healthier era. Some hotels lay on a big breakfast buffet for their guests, with everything from cornflakes to omelets. At lunch and dinner the proceedings often start with a filling soup. The most typical is *caldo verde* (green soup), a thick broth of shredded kale, potato purée and perhaps a chunk of sausage. Another soupy starter, a summery idea, is *gaspacho*, the Portuguese interpretation of the Andalusian "liquid salad", a cold soup featuring tomatoes, cucumbers and peppers.

Fish and Shellfish

The atmosphere means a lot, so if you're on a beach or quayside the *sardinhas assadas* (grilled sardines) can make a memorable lunch. A salad of lettuce, onion and green pepper and a slice of homemade bread round out the fisherman's treat.

Bigger fish like sole, mullet and bream are also grilled, or in some recipes boiled. When fish reach the size of tunny or swordfish, they're sliced into steaks and grilled or broiled in tasty casseroles. If you're looking for swordfish, the word is *espadarte* or *peixe agulha*. Not to be confused with *peixe espada* (scabbard fish), a thin, sinister-looking giant so long it has to be folded to fit in the fishermen's trays.

And then there is *bacalhau*, the dried, salted codfish from cold northern waters, an acquired taste. A couple of weeks in Portugal may not be sufficient to learn to love it, but you ought to try it for the experience.

Seafood restaurants usually have the latest trophies on display—lobster, crab, oysters, cockles, clams, prawns, squid—so you can point to what you fancy.

More Main Dishes

The Algarve's most innovative dish is *amêijoas na cataplana,* baby clams with sausage, ham, onion, tomato, garlic, paprika and white wine cooked and served in a sort of pressure-cooker called a *cataplana.*

Xarém owes its name, and presumably the approximate recipe, to the Moorish occupation. It's a hearty casserole of cornmeal, clams, bacon, ham and slices of sausage, with white wine.

Feijoada is a stew of white beans and cabbage with sausage, bacon and pork bits, a restrained version of Brazil's sumptuous national dish.

Frango—chicken—is popular, barbecued on a spit or enlivened with *piri-piri* sauce, a peppery echo of Portugal's African possessions.

Cabrito means kid, or young goat. *Cabrito estufado* is a stew of kid and onions, tomatoes, potatoes and peas. *Cabrito assado* or *no forno* is baked kid, perhaps with a wine sauce.

Generally the portions served in Portuguese restaurants are enormous. They are often garnished with both rice and potatoes.

Happy Endings

Portuguese sweets are so sweet they must set some sort of record. Almonds, figs and eggs usually figure in the recipes, along with loads of sugar or honey. Occasionally chocolate, cinnamon, orange or a type of pumpkin add to the flavour.

An old Bolshevik is inexplicably honoured in an extravagantly rich dessert called *pudim Molotov,* involving an egg-white mousse and caramel sauce.

For less overwhelming desserts, try *pudim flan,* a caramel custard, or *arroz doce,* a rice pudding sprinkled with cinnamon.

Fruit desserts include *compota,* a mixture of stewed fruits, and *maçã assada,* baked apple. Or take your fruit fresh—*laranjas* (oranges), *ananás* (pineapple) or *bananas,* according to season.

If cheese is offered, look for *Serra da Estrela,* a rich ewe's milk cheese still made by traditional methods. Out of season *Tipo Serra* is a substitute. Light, creamy *Queijo Fresco* is sometimes served as an appetizer.

Wines

The Portuguese word for "bottle" is *garrafa.* If you want a carafe of the house wine, don't fall for this "false friend"; ask for *um frasco.* Other than that, all you have to know is *tinto* (red), *branco*

Scenery rivals the cataplana and ingredients at a restaurant in Porches.

(white) and maybe *rosé. Vinho verde,* the slightly sparkling young white wine from northern Portugal, served cool, enhances seafood.

The local beers are refreshing on a hot day. Or you can drink mineral water, fruit juice or international brands of soft drinks.

Coffee Time

Coffee-loving Portuguese have a small, black expresso to wind up lunch or dinner. The word is *bica.* A *bica* with a little milk in it is called a *garoto.* If you prefer a full-sized café-au-lait—white coffee in a glass—ask for a *galão.* You can also order *chá* (tea).

When and Where

Meal times in Portugal follow general European patterns, meaning that they are earlier than in neighbouring Spain. Lunch can be served at any time from 12.30 to 2.30 p.m., and dinner from 7.30 to 9.30 p.m. (Across the border in Andalusia they're just starting to think about dinner at 9.30 or 10 p.m.) Restaurants are officially rated in four categories: luxury, 1st, 2nd and 3rd class. Don't turn up your nose at a 3rd class restaurant with paper tablecloths; the ratings are based on the facilities available, not the quality of the food.

Bom apetite!

55

$Sports$

The climate helps. In the Algarve the sun is almost always shining when you need it—3,000 hours a year. For most holiday-makers that means water sports, but beyond the bountiful beaches there's a world of opportunities for golfers, tennis players, horsemen and many others.

Golf, Anyone?

The Algarve is the most golf-blessed corner of Europe, with courses enough to keep any discerning fan busy for more than a fortnight. The landscaping, by famous course designers, can take your breath away, or cost you a ball in the ocean.

Some of the finest championship courses are attached to the major resort complexes, such as Vilamoura and Quinta do Lago. Holiday-makers staying in hotels, apartments or villas in these resorts thus have easy access to the links, sometimes as part of the package deal. Other hotels advertise specially reduced green fees at nearby clubs. You may need a handicap certificate.

Tennis, Too

Ever more tennis players are coming to the Algarve to perfect their game. Seizing the opportunity, some well known tennis personalities have become involved in coaching at specially designed tennis centres along the coast. Many courts have flood-lighting for play in the cooler hours. For tennis fans who take the game less seriously, many hotels have courts just for fun, with tuition optional. You can rent equipment.

Horse Riding

The scenery and the climate attract horsemen year-round. Most of the Algarve's stables are along the coast starting west of Faro, where the terrain becomes more dramatic. The specialities range from pony rides for children to show-jumping advice for experienced equestrians. And there are treks along the beaches or through the pine forests.

Water Sports

Forty-five Algarve beaches have been awarded European blue

You don't have to be a champion to pursue golf at Quinta do Lago.

flags of distinction—that's more than half of all the beaches so honoured in Portugal. They start at Odeceixe on the south-west coast and run all the way east to Monte Gordo, the endless sandy stretch near the Spanish border. The cliff-backed beaches of the west are more spectacular, but swimming is safer for children, and the ocean is warmer, on the eastern part of the coast. Even the remote coves usually have a beach bar or restaurant.

Windsurfing experts gravitate to the ocean-facing west coast, but resorts on quieter seas—ideal for beginners—have boards for hire and instructors on call.

Scuba diving offers dramatic possibilities among the underwater caves and mysterious rock formations of the western coast. Equipment and instruction are available at many resorts.

If you want to make waves, you can water-ski (the sea is more dependable in the lagoons) or jet-ski at some of the long beaches.

Renting a dinghy is no problem at several resorts; for a bigger vessel, crewed or uncrewed, try the Algarve's prime marina, Vilamoura.

Deep-sea fishing expeditions are a speciality at the quayside in Portimão and at Vilamoura. 57

The Hard Facts

Climate

It's mostly delightful in the Algarve, even "out of season". With its vaunted 3,000 hours of sunshine per year, the region is Portugal's warmest and driest. In July and August the average number of rainy days is zero, with the average maximum temperature in the upper 20s C (the low 80s F). It rarely gets uncomfortably hot. At the other end of the scale, in December and January, when you have a one-in-three chance of being rained on, the average minimum temperature is around 10°C (50°F). Ocean temperatures are not quite up to Mediterranean standards, but close enough on the south-facing beaches.

Health

Conditions of hygiene are good, so the only thing to worry about is an overdose of sunshine. You can avoid sunburn and worse by confining your beach outings to the hours when the sun is low in the sky, applying sunscreen, and wearing a hat and a shirt when possible. Like the sun, the powerful local wine and spirits should also be taken in moderation. Tap water in the cities is officially safe to drink, but you'd do better to consume bottled mineral water.

For small problems—like mosquito bites or queasy stomach—consult any pharmacy. Chemists *(farmácias)* are open during normal business hours; after hours a *farmácia de serviço* stays open late. The address is found in the newspaper or by the door of any other pharmacy.

For more serious ailments or injuries, ask at your hotel or the tourist office for a list of English-speaking doctors, or go to the nearest hospital. Portugal has reciprocal health agreements with most European countries. Visitors presenting UK passports are entitled to free in-patient treatment in officially designated hospitals; other European Union nationals must present form E111. There are also private medical and dental clinics in the Algarve.

What to Pack

In spring, summer and autumn you can travel light. Except for a pullover, which you might need on a summer evening, the only season requiring a substantial sweater or a light coat would be winter. But do pack serious walking shoes if you're planning to go beyond the beach to wander cobbled streets and country paths.

Anything you forgot to pack can normally be found in the Algarve's shops. But if you take prescription medicines, it's wise to pack all you need; it may not be easy to track down the Portuguese equivalent in the correct dosage.

Luxury hotels and restaurants don't discourage a touch of formality, but the general rule is casual dress. Don't overdo it: swimsuits are inappropriate in towns, and if you visit a historic church it's only proper to dress on the sober side.

Formalities

Visitors from most countries require only a valid passport, with no visa, to enter Portugal. National identity cards are sufficient for most European nationals, and citizens of the UK can use a British Visitors Passport. Visitors from beyond Europe have to fill in arrival and departure cards to present to the authorities. There are no limits on the amount of Portuguese or foreign currency in cash or traveller's cheques you can bring into Portugal. On the way out, the limit is normally 100,000 escudos in local currency or the equivalent of a million escudos in foreign currency.

Airport

Faro International Airport, which receives millions of passengers a year, has a huge modern terminal with a cheerful, simulated tropical atmosphere involving a welcoming colour scheme of canary yellow, blue and pink, and lots of glass. It has all the usual amenities—free baggage trolleys, information desks, car hire counters, bars, restaurants, shops, and a bank and post office. The airport is only 7 km (4 miles) west of the provincial capital, Faro.

Transport

Buses, most of them comfortable, link all the main towns and resorts of the Algarve. Timetables are posted at tourist offices and bus stations. There are also modern air-conditioned coaches to Lisbon.

Portuguese Railways (CP) serve much of the Algarve, though some of the stations are far away from town centres. There are reduced fares for children and a Senior Citizen rate for people over 65, and various money-saving fares valid for unlimited travel.

All the towns and resorts have taxi service. Cabs await clients at ranks and hotels. They can also

59

be summoned by telephone. In areas where meters are unused or non-existent there are flat rates for standard journeys; it's prudent to ask the fare in advance.

Communications

Telephone calls from hotel rooms tend to be seductively convenient but very expensive, as most hotels add prohibitive surcharges, even if automatic dialling bypasses their operators. If money is a factor, use public telephones instead. To avoid the inconvenience of stacking up coins, buy a phone card at a news-stand or post office. You can also make calls at post offices, where you phone first and pay later. In resorts you may come across privately-operated telephone offices with similar facilities. Calls abroad start with 00 followed by the country code, area code and the number of the subscriber. For incoming calls, Portugal's country code is 351.

Postal service. The post office *(CTT* or *Correios)* is open from 9 a.m. to 6 or 7 p.m., Monday to Friday; some close for lunch. Those in Faro and Portimão and at the airport also operate Saturday mornings until 12.30 p.m. If all you need are stamps, you can buy them wherever postcards are sold. Post boxes are bright red, and many are in the form of British pillar boxes.

Fax. The bigger hotels have fax machines. They are also available at telephone service bureaux.

Complaints

If you have a serious grievance in a hotel or restaurant that can't be solved by face-to-face contact, ask for the *livro de reclamações,* the official complaint book. This gesture alone is likely to speed a solution, for the manager of any establishment would be reluctant to have a complaint forwarded to the tourism authorities. In any case, the first step is to ask to see whoever's in charge and calmly explain your problem.

Social graces

First, remember where you are: Portugal is proud of its identity and its differences from its giant neighbour. Thus, saying *gracias* in Spanish (instead of the Portuguese *obrigado*) won't make you any friends. Saying *bom dia* before starting any conversation in any language will warm the atmosphere.

"Old-fashioned politeness" is prescribed for all contacts with the Portuguese. A lot of handshaking goes on.

Visitors from countries where smokers have been doomed to ostracism and repression may be surprised to find that Portugal still smokes up a storm—in restaurants, cafés, offices, hotel lobbies and in the street. But smoking is prohibited on buses and in cinemas and theatres.

Religion

The overwhelming majority of Portuguese are Catholics, who tend to go to church on Sunday and are swept up in the religious festivals that punctuate the year. But it's a free and tolerant country, and minority sects are unhampered.

Foreign visitors are catered for in the Algarve, where Catholic and Protestant services in English and other languages are prominently announced on the bulletin boards of tourist offices and hotels.

Police

In Algarve resorts, police wearing armbands marked "CD" (meaning local corps) are there to help tourists; they probably have some knowledge of foreign languages.

Highway patrols are run by the *Guarda Nacional Republicana* (GNR), often in pairs on high-powered motorcycles.

Crime

Car hire companies strongly advise their customers to close windows and lock all doors, leave no valuables visible and nothing of importance in the boot. They also recommend parking in secure car parks, especially at night. The risk of car theft, or break-ins, is concentrated at beaches and other spots where cars may be out of sight for a time.

In the resorts it's wise to keep all valuables in safe deposit boxes; some hotels and apartment complexes have them in the rooms, or the reception desk can take responsibility.

Although burglaries are now a fact of Algarve life, violent crime is still very unusual.

Emergencies

For police, fire or ambulance service, the all-purpose emergency number to dial from anywhere in Portugal is 115. In more complex cases, consult your consulate.

Driving

Many roads have been greatly improved in the region, and a fully-fledged motorway now runs from the border with southern Spain across half of the Algarve before veering north towards Lisbon.

Driving conditions are standard for Europe: drive on the right, overtake on the left, wear seat belts, don't drink and drive. Unless otherwise marked, speed limits are 120 kph (75 mph) on the motorway, 90 kph (55 mph) 61 on other highways, and 50 kph (31 mph) in built-up areas. Portuguese drivers, who don't always take the speed limits seriously, have a reputation as accident prone. Another hazard is the foreign driver baffled by the road signs. Beware, too, of unconventional traffic. Farm tractors venturing onto highways now must be equipped with a twirling light like an emergency vehicle, but sheep and donkeys are as dangerous as ever.

Parking is difficult in town centres. Some have installed parking meters, but these don't seem to discourage all-day parkers. You may come across ticket dispensers, with instructions printed in Portuguese and English. Display the valid ticket inside your windscreen.

Renting a car is straightforward, with local and internationally-known firms competing at the airport and in the resorts. The differences in tariffs tend to be very small. Unless you pay with an internationally accepted credit card you'll have to put down a large deposit.

Language

The national language is Portuguese, one of the world's most widely spoken tongues—from Brazil to Mozambique and Macau. If you know one of the Romance languages, you'll prob-

ably be able to understand the signs, perhaps even read the newspaper headlines. Wherever tourists gather, English is known (and German and to a lesser extent French).

Opening hours

Banks are usually open from 8.30 a.m. to 3 p.m., Monday to Friday. Post offices operate from 9 a.m. to 6 or 7 p.m.; smaller ones may take a lunch break. Shops and offices are open from 9 a.m. to 1 p.m. and again from 3 to 7 p.m. Big shopping centres stay open later. Museums are generally open from 10 a.m. to 5 p.m. daily except Mondays and public holidays.

Holidays and festivals

Fixed public holidays are:

New Year's Day	1 January
Liberty Day	25 April
Labour Day	1 May
Portugal Day	10 June
Assumption	15 August
Republic Day	5 October
All Saints' Day	1 November
Independence Day	1 December
Immaculate Conception	8 December
Christmas	25 December

Moveable feasts: Shrove Tuesday, Good Friday, Corpus Christi. In addition, every town celebrates its own saint's day with everything from religious processions to fireworks.

Time

Although it's on the same westerly longitude as Ireland, Portugal has adopted Central European Time in order to align itself more firmly with the European Union. Like Paris and Brussels, then, Portugal is on GMT + 1 in winter and GMT + 2 in summer.

Currency

The national currency is the *escudo* (abbreviated esc.) which means shield. Banknotes come in denominations from 100 to 10,000 escudos. (The sum of one thousand escudos is known as a *conto*.) Coins are minted in denominations from 1 to 200 escudos. Note that prices are usually written with a dollar sign instead of a decimal point: 10,000$00 means 10,000 escudos.

Traveller's cheques and Eurocheques can be cashed at banks and exchange offices, and there are 24-hour automatic cash machines which dispense escudos billed to your home bank or credit card.

Tipping

Whenever there's any doubt, 10 per cent is a reasonable tip for service personnel, from hairdressers to waiters and taxi drivers. And don't forget to give a few coins to hotel maids and porters.

Toilets

Look for the signs WC *Senhoras* (ladies) and WC *Homens* (men). Otherwise, your best bet is the nearest hotel, restaurant or café (order at least a coffee).

Newspapers

Leading European dailies and magazines are sold in all the tourist centres, in all the languages of these cosmopolitan resorts.

Broadcasting

Portugal's four television channels show films and telefilms in the original language with Portuguese subtitles. In addition, many hotels offer their guests foreign channels via satellite. Some local stations schedule programmes in English and French aimed at tourists.

Photography

All the popular types of film are available at photo shops, newsstands and souvenir shops. Twenty-four-hour processing is standard. Remember to keep cameras and film out of the hot sun.

Voltage

The standard electric current in Portugal is 220 volt 50 cycles AC, using round pins as elsewhere on the Continent. American appliances require transformers and plug adaptors.

INDEX

Series editor: Barbara Ender
Photos: Bernard Joliat, Claude Huber, A.G.E. FotoStock
Design: Dominique Michellod, Corsier/Vevey
Maps: Falk-Verlag, Hamburg, p.4–5 JPM Publications

The
PORTUGUESE
Way

Olá!
Hello!

J·P·M A handy guide with everyday phrases and vital
information to help you enjoy your stay in Portugal.

Olá! Hello!

The Portuguese are a friendly people. They will appreciate it if you greet them with an *"olá!"* ("hello") or *"Olá, como está?"* ("Hello, how are you?") which is a unisex greeting. Expect to be told how the person is, sometimes in detail.

On second acquaintance you may start kissing people on the face (do not smack; once is enough). If you are a woman, present your left cheek to be kissed. If you are a man, peck the lady on whichever cheek she presents. If you meet an old lady, make a gesture of kissing her hand.

Your answer to the same question (how are you?) can be: *"Bem, obrigado"* (or *"obrigada"* if you are a woman), ("Well, thank you") though a true Portuguese will probably reply *"Vai-se andando"*, ("We're plodding along"). The Portuguese are polite, but not necessarily optimistic; their national song, the *fado,* means "fate" and dwells on the mournful side of life.

Upon taking your leave, say *"Adeus"* ("Good-bye") even if you are seeing the person again tomorrow, or *"Até logo"* ("See you later").

"Bom dia" is "Good day" (you say it in the morning), *"Boa tarde"* ("Good afternoon") in the afternoon and evening, or *"Boa noite"* (Good evening). These expressions serve as greetings, too, but in this case should be followed by *"Tá bom?"* or *"Como está?"* anyway.

Don't be shy: To help you with your spoken Portuguese we provide a very simple transcription alongside the phrases. You may not end up sounding like a native but people will be pleased that you're trying. Portuguese has a few sounds that are hard to pronounce, for instance anything with *"ão"* in it. Our transcription represents any nasal sound by underlining the vowel, for instance não = <u>now</u>. Some syllables must be stressed, and these are printed in capital letters.

Hello.	Olá.	oh-LAH
Good morning.	Bom dia.	bo DEE-uh
Good afternoon.	Boa tarde.	BOH-uh TAHR-duh
Good evening.	Boa noite.	BOH-uh NOY-tuh
Goodbye.	Adeus.	uh-DEH-oosh
See you later.	Até logo.	uh-TEH LOH-goo
Yes/No.	Sim/Não.	see/now
Maybe.	Talvez.	tahl-VAYSH
That's fine/Okay.	Está bem.	ish-TAH bay
That's right!	Certo!	SEHR-too
Please.	Por favor.	poor fuh-VOHR
Thank you/Thanks.	Obrigado/-da.	oh-bri-GAH-doo/-duh
Thank you very much.	Muito obrigado/-da.	MOOI-too oh-bri-GAH-doo/-duh
You're welcome.	De nada.	duh NAH-duh
Nice to meet you.	Prazer em conhecê-lo/la.	pruh-ZAYR ay koon-yuh-SAY loo/luh
How are you?	Como está?	KOH-moo ish-TAH
Well, thanks.	Bem, obrigado/-da.	bay oh-bri-GAH-doo/-duh.
And you?	E você?	ee voh-SAY
Pardon me.	Desculpe.	dish-KOOL-puh
I'm (very) sorry.	Peço imensa desculpa.	PEH-soo ee-MAY-suh dish-KOOL-puh
Don't mention it.	Não tem de quê.	now tay duh kay
Excuse me.	Com licença.	ko lee-SAY-suh
My name is...	Chamo-me...	SHUH-moo muh
I don't understand.	Não percebo.	now puhr-SAY-boo
Slowly, please.	Devagar, por favor.	duh-vuh-GAHR poor fuh-VOHR
Could you say that again, please?	Importa-se de repetir, por favor?	ee-POHR-tuh suh duh ruh-puh-TEER poor fuh-VOHR
Do you speak English?	Fala inglês?	FAH-luh ee-GLAYSH
Let's go.	Vamos.	VUH-moosh

Táxi!   Taxi!

Taking a taxi is like drawing a lottery. Cleanliness, courtesy, competence, honesty and safety vary. Some drivers are angelic, others less so.

In Portugal, taxis are painted green and black; a few are a light shade of beige. On top, they have a rectangular sign appropriately saying "TÁXI" with a green light on each side. If both lights are out and the "TÁXI" sign light is on, it is free.

Taxis can be flagged down in the street; there are taxi stands, but mostly they are empty. Some are reliable, such as the one in the Rossio (downtown Lisbon). Taxis are plentiful at the airport, the train stations and bus terminals. They'll charge you a bit more for transporting your bags. You can also summon a *rádio-táxi* or *tele-táxi* by phone.

Public transportation. In Portugal, a bus is called an *"autocarro"* if it runs within the city limits. A long distance bus changes from masculine to feminine and becomes a *"camionete de carreira"*. Enter a bus by the front door, pay, get a ticket and punch it. If you do not have the exact amount, the driver can make change. To leave, press the STOP button and get out by the back door. Bus stops are plentiful and orange-colored.

Metro(politano) — Lisbon only. Pronounced *"MEH-troo"*, the subway opens at 6 a.m. and closes at 1:30 a.m. It is reasonably punctual and reasonably comfortable. When you get down to the *metro,* you'll see an orange-colored machine. Punch a button, the price of the ticket appears, insert coins in a slot and you'll get your ticket and change.

Trains and trams. From Lisbon to Sintra and to Cascais you can take a moderately priced train. Avoid the rush hours. Lisbon and some other cities have streetcars *(eléctricos).* They are quaint, poetic and slow, though reasonably clean and safe. You enter, buy a ticket and depart just as in the bus.

Taxi, please!	Um táxi, se faz favor!	<u>oo</u> TAH-ksee suh fahsh fuh-VOHR
Are you free?	Está livre?	ish-TAH LEE-vruh
To the Hotel Central.	Para o Hotel Central.	PAH-ruh oo oh-TEHL s<u>ay</u>-TRAHL
To the airport/ station, please.	Para o aeroporto/ estação, por favor.	PAH-ruh oo uh-eh-roh-POHR-too/ish-tuh-S<u>OW</u> poor fuh-VOHR
I'm in a hurry.	Estou com pressa.	ish-TOH k<u>o</u> PREH-suh
Please stop here.	Por favor pare aqui.	poor fuh-VOHR PAH-ruh uh-KEE
Please wait for me.	Por favor espere por mim.	poor fuh-VOHR ish-PEH-ruh poor m<u>ee</u>
How much is it?	Quanto é?	KW<u>A</u>-too eh
Keep the change.	Guarde o troco.	GWAHR-duh oo TROH-koo
Where is the subway, please?	Onde é o metro, por favor?	<u>O</u>-duh eh oo MEH-troo poor fuh-VOHR
one way	só de ida	soh duh EE-duh
round-trip	de ida e volta	duh EE-duh ee VOHL-tuh
first class	primeira classe	pree-MAY-ruh KLAH-suh
second class	segunda classe	suh-G<u>OO</u>-duh KLAH-suh
Is this seat free?	Esta lugar está livre?	AYSH-tuh loo-GAHR ish-TAH LEE-vruh

You and you. There are many forms of "you" in Portuguese and getting them right is a bit of a puzzle. *Tu* may be used for addressing children, close friends, family. *Você* may be the same, but can also be used for addressing servants and people with whom you are less familiar (though some people use it to address their husbands/wives/children etc). *O senhor* and *a senhora* are for strangers or as a deferential manner of addressing older and respectable people in the third person. If you are addressing anybody with a university degree you'll want to say *Senhor Doutor* or *Senhora Doutora*.

A minha chave, por favor!
My key, please!

People working at the desk of your hotel are bound to know a foreign language. But it's always agreeable to offer a phrase or two in Portuguese. Dealing with the chambermaid you'll probably have to rely on Portuguese and sign language. Tip the bellhop when he carries your bags and the maid if you stay for several days, but there's no need to tip the desk people, unless they solve a particularly tricky problem for you. They are generally quite helpful.

Hotels are rated from one to five stars and *Luxo* (Luxury). There are also *residenciais* (smaller, residential hotels which can be quite nice and much less expensive) and *pensões* (lower in the comfort scale); unlike the French *pension*, sometimes they provide no meals except breakfast. In Portugal, a continental breakfast is often included in the price of a room, but you'd better make sure.

You can stay at the *pousadas,* which are government-run and sometimes located in beautiful palaces and old convents. They are not terribly expensive; best make a reservation, as they have few rooms. While driving around the country, take advantage of *turismo de habitação* (house tourism). Spread around the country there is a network of old manors and comfortable houses whose owners rent out rooms to help with their upkeep. You can get the information booklet at the tourist office.

That's entertainment. Aside from the usual range of night-clubs, discos and bars, a very Portuguese night out may be spent in a *fado* house. There you can listen to the soulful traditional music of the country—songs of despair, nostalgia, longing. You don't have to know the language to be moved.

Here's the confirmation/voucher.	Tem aqui a confirmação/o *voucher*.	tay ah-KEE uh ko-feer-muh-SOW/ oo "voucher"
a single room	um quarto *single*	oo KWAHR-too "single"
a double	um duplo	oo DOO-ploo
twin beds	duas camas	DOO-uhsh KUH-muhsh
double bed	cama de casal	KUH-muh duh kuh-ZAHL
with a bath/shower	com banheiro/chuveiro	ko buh-NYAY-roo/shoo-VAY-roo
My key, please.	A minha chave, por favor.	uh MEE-nyuh SHAH-vuh poor fuh-VOHR
Is there mail for me?	Tem correio para mim?	tay koo-RAY-oo PUH-ruh mee
I need: hangers	Preciso de cabides	pruh-SEE-zoo duh kuh-BEE-duhsh
soap	sabonete	suh-boo-NAY-tuh
a blanket	um cobertor	oo koo-buhr-TOHR
a different pillow	outro travesseiro	oh-TROO trah-vay-SAY-roo
These are clothes to be washed.	Estas roupas são para lavar.	EHSH-tuhsh ROH-puhsh sow PUH-ruh luh-VAHR
These are clothes to be cleaned / pressed.	Estas roupas são para limpar/ passar a ferro.	EHSH-tuhsh ROH-puhsh sow PUH-ruh lee-PAHR/ puh-SAHR uh FEH-roo
Urgently.	É urgente.	eh oor-ZHAY-tuh
I'm checking out.	Vou-me embora.	VOH-muh ay-BOH-ruh
I'd like to pay by credit card.	Gostaria de pagar com cartão de crédito.	goosh-tah-REE-uh duh pah-GAHR ko kuhr-TOW duh KREH-dee-too

---

Tips. Around ten percent is the accepted tipping scale. The scale drops as the price goes up, which means that if you get a 10,000 escudos bill for whatever it is, it is all right to give 750 escudos. On taxis, round up the bill; if it is 430, give 450.

Bom proveito! *Enjoy it!*

The Portuguese love to eat and drink. With the exception of breakfast, which is light if it exists at all, meals tend to be on the heavy side. Do not come to the country with the idea of losing weight or maintaining the weight you've got. Food is good and plentiful; sweets are very sweet, cheeses spicy.

Wine is a national passion and besides red, white and rosé there is a fourth variety, the so-called green wine, a young, semi-sparkling white that goes splendidly with seafood. People eat two main meals a day: lunch (around 1 p. m. or *13 horas*) and dinner (around 8 p. m. or *20 horas*).

There's a national unanimity about *bacalhau* (codfish) being delicious; it is said that there are 1,000 ways of cooking codfish, so no wonder it is on every menu. *Bacalhau* is an acquired taste, but do try it. When in season (late spring and summer) fresh grilled sardines are very popular, as are roasted chestnuts sold in the streets during the fall.

Besides restaurants, *cervejarias* (beer halls) are convivial places full of customers consuming large quantities of beer accompanied by salted *tremoços* (lupine seeds). You can have meals there, especially fresh seafood or a steak, until two o'clock in the morning and sometimes later. The Portuguese think nothing of going to sleep on a full stomach.

Coffee is drunk at all hours, very strong, black and sweet. Served in a small cup, it is called a *bica;* with a few drops of milk it's a *garoto.*

Friends indeed. In the upper class restaurants you'll find menus in English. Elsewhere you'll probably have to depend upon our mini-vocabulary or the kindness of strangers, but generally people will be helpful. They enjoy suggesting food and wine; take their advice.

I'm hungry/thirsty.	**Tenho fome/sede.**	TAY-nyoo FOH-muh/ SAY-duh
A table for two, please.	**Uma mesa para duas pessoas, por favor.**	OO-muh MAY-zuh PUH-ruh DOO-uhsh puh-SOH-uhsh poor fuh-VOHR
The menu, please.	**A carta, por favor.**	uh KAHR-tuh poor fuh-VOHR
The fixed menu, please.	**O menu turístico, por favor.**	oo muh-NOO too-REES-tee-koo poor fuh-VOHR
I'm a vegetarian.	**Sou vegetariano.**	soh vuh-zhuh-tuh-RYUH-noo
The wine list, please.	**A carta dos vinhos, por favor.**	uh KAHR-tuh doosh VEE-nyoosh poor fuh-VOHR
A bottle of red/white/ rosé/green wine.	**Uma garrafa de vinho tinto/branco/ rosé/verde.**	OO-muh guh-RAH-fuh duh VEE-nyoo TEE-too/BRA-koo/ roh-ZAY/VAYR-duh
beef	**bife**	BEE-fuh
bread	**pão**	pow
butter	**manteiga**	ma-TAY-guh
cheese	**queijo**	KAY-zhoo
chicken	**frango**	FRA-goo
coffee	**café**	kuh-FEH
fish	**peixe**	PAY-shuh
meat	**carne**	KAHR-nuh
fruit	**fruta**	FROO-tuh
ice cream	**gelado**	zhuh-LAH-doo
milk	**leite**	LAY-tuh
mineral water	**água mineral**	AH-gwuh mee-nuh-RAHL
pork	**carne de porco**	KAHR-nuh duh POHR-koo
salt and pepper	**sal e pimenta**	sahl ee pee-MAY-tuh
tea	**chá**	shah
The check, please.	**A conta, por favor.**	uh KO-tuh poor fuh-VOHR

Está lá?   *Are you there?*

When you dial a phone number and somebody picks up the phone at the other end, he or she will not say "hello" but *"Estou?"* ("Am I here?"). You reply: *"Tá? Tá lá?"* ("Are? Are you there?"). The other person confirms: *"Tou, Tou."* ("I am, I am."). You may proceed with the conversation.

Before hanging up, some people will say: *"Com licença."* ("By your leave" or "Excuse me."). Extra-polite, but it's not recommended.

To call collect, dial **098.** You can use a variety of phone cards, which you can buy in Lisbon and Porto. You will pay more if you phone from the hotel than in a normal phone booth.

To call the U.S. and Canada direct, dial 001, then the area code without the initial 0, then the subscriber's number. For the U.K., the country code is 0044.

Post office. Square red signs with a horse-rider logo identify the offices of *CTT or Correios,* generally open from 9 a.m. to 6 p.m. Some close for lunch. Lisbon's Restauradores office closes at 10 p.m. and the airport's never closes. Stamps can also be bought at certain tobacconists'. Mailboxes are red. Fax machines are available in most hotels.

Number, please: A Lisbon phone number is always preceded by **01,** unless you are calling from within the city; Porto is **02,** and so on. Phone numbers are spoken one at a time: two four seven, three one one nine (247 3119).
But to start at the beginning:

1 um	5 cinco	9 nove	13 treze	17 dezassete
2 dois	6 seis	10 dez	14 catorze	18 dezoito
3 três	7 sete	11 onze	15 quinze	19 dezanove
4 quatro	8 oito	12 doze	16 dezasseis	20 vinte

May I use this phone?	Posso usar este telefone?	POH-soo oo-ZAHR AYSH-tuh tuh-luh-FOH-nuh
Can I reverse the charges?	Posso ligar a cobrar?	POH-soo lee-GAHR uh koo-BRAHR
Wrong number.	É engano.	eh ay-GAH-noo
Speak more slowly, please.	Fale mais devagar, por favor.	FAH-luh mighsh duh-vuh-GAHR poor fuh-VOHR
Could you take a message?	Pode tomar note de um recado?	POH-duh too-MAHR NOH-tuh duh oo ruh-KAH-doo
My number is…	O meu número é o…	oo MEH-oo NOO-muh-roo eh oo
My room number is…	O número do meu quarto é o…	oo NOO-muh-roo doo MEH-oo KWAHR-too eh oo
Do you sell stamps?	Vende selos?	VAY-duh SAY-loosh
I'd like to mail this parcel.	Queria enviar esta encomenda.	kuh-REE-uh ay-VYAHR EHSH-tuh ay-koo-MAY-duh
Can I send a fax?	Posso mandar um fax?	POH-soo ma-DAHR oo fahks
Where's the mailbox?	Onde é o marco do correio?	O-duh eh oo MAHR-koo doo koo-RAY-oo
registered letter	carta registada	KAHR-tuh ruh-zhish-TAH-duh
air mail	por avião	poor uh-VYOW
postcard	cartão postal	kuhr-TOW poosh-TAHL

Happy Talk: Build up your vocabulary with a few useful, cheery adjectives: *giro* (nice), *óptimo* (fine), *estupendo* (great), *imenso* (meaning *a lot*). The Portuguese have a tendency to sprinkle their conversation with interjections such as *pois* (an agreement), *pá, eh pá* (as Americans might say "man, hey man") and *ena pá* (this conveys a sensation of surprise, awe, excitement).

Quanto é? *How much is it?*

The *escudo* (the shield, literally) is the unit of currency. It is divided in 100 *centavos* (known familiarly as *tostões*). The largest bill is 10,000 escudos; then there are the 5,000, 2,000, 1,000 and 500 *escudos* bills. Coins come in denominations of 200, 100, 50, 20, 10, 5, 2.50, 1 *escudo* and 50 *centavos*. The 50 *escudos* coin is the largest in diameter, the 1 *escudo* the smallest.

Hotels usually change foreign currency or traveler's checks into Portuguese *escudos* but the exchange rate is less generous than at a bank. Most banks are open from 8:30 a.m. to 3:30 p.m. Monday to Friday. Always take along your passport when changing money. (You can also make use of bank cash machines linked up with your bank or credit card. You must have a 4-digit PIN number.)

Do make use of downtown Duty Free Shops that allow you to get refunds for the VAT (if you are a traveler from outside the European Union) at the airport when you leave. Pack these purchases in a carry-on bag, instead of checking them in, in case the officer demands to see your purchases. These shops are easily identified by a banner hanging outside. If there is no banner, ask anyway; sometimes a small hamlet away from Lisbon has Duty Free Shopping, and sometimes shipping too.

Shopping, from first rate porcelain and Arraiolos rugs to gold and silver filigree and port wine, is one of the pleasures of Portugal.

Credit cards of the big international firms are widely accepted in hotels, restaurants and stores.

Shops are generally open 9 a.m. to 1 p.m. and 3 p.m. to 7 p.m. Except for the big department stores and malls they will probably be closed Saturday afternoons and Sundays.

currency	dinheiro	dee-NYAY-roo
exchange	câmbio	KA-byoo
Where can I change money?	Onde posso trocar dinheiro?	O-duh POH-soo troo-KAHR dee-NYAY-roo
bank	banco	BA-koo
Can you cash a traveler's check?	Pode trocar-me um traveler's check?	POH-duh troo-KAHR muh oo "traveler's check"
I want to change dollars.	Quero trocar dólares.	KEH-roo troo-KAHR DOH-luhsh
Will this credit card do?	Aceita este cartão de crédito?	uh-SAY-tuh AYSH-tuh kuhr-TOW duh KREH-dee-too
Just looking...	Estou só a ver...	ish-TOH soh uh vayr
How much is this?	Quanto custa isto?	KWA-too KOOSH-tuh ISH-too
cheap	barato	buh-RAH-too
expensive	caro	KAH-roo
Can I try it on?	Posso provar?	POH-soo proo-VAHR
I don't know the European sizes.	Não conheço as medidas europeas.	now koo-NYAY-soo uhsh muh-DEE-duhsh eh-oo-roo-PAY-uhsh
I'll think about it.	Vou pensar.	voh pa-SAHR
I'll buy it.	Vou comprar.	voh ko-PRAHR
It's a gift.	É para oferta.	eh PUH-ruh oo-FEHR-tuh
A receipt, please.	Uma factura, por favor.	OO-muh fuhk-TOO-ruh poor fuh-VOHR
antique shop	antiquário	a-tee-KWAH-ryoo
bakery	padaria	puh-duh-REE-uh
mall	centro comercial	SAY-troo koo-muhr-SYAHL
pharmacy	farmácia	fuhr-MAH-syuh
supermarket	supermercado	soo-pehr-muhr-KAH-doo
jewelry store	ourivesaria	oh-ree-vuh-zuh-REE-uh
pastry shop	pastelaria	puhsh-tuh-luh-REE-uh
delicatessen	charcutaria	shuhr-koo-tah-REE-uh
market	mercado	muhr-KAH-doo

Socorro!   *Help!*

The best-planned vacation can sometimes be spoiled for health reasons. It doesn't take much—perhaps over-enthusiasm in sampling the green wine—but you must know where to turn. For small health problems, look for the green cross identifying a *farmácia* (pharmacy). They are open from 9 a.m. to 1 p.m. and 3 p.m. to 7 p.m. Late-night and all-night pharmacies are listed in the daily papers. You can also go to any pharmacy and read the address of the nearest open pharmacy in a lighted panel by the door. If your malady worsens, ask the hotel desk to get you a doctor or point you to the nearest hospital. In an emergency, dial **115.**

Safety first. As in any city, don't take needless risks. Leave your valuables in the hotel safe *(cofre)*. Don't walk around with all your money in your wallet, glittering jewelry and your passport in a vulnerable handbag. Keep them separate and carry only the money you are going to need. If you are driving a car, put your belongings out of sight when you park it. Women shouldn't walk around the old quarters by themselves, especially at night; book a tour.

Police. Although most Portuguese *polícias* (policemen) do not speak English, they do try to be helpful to tourists. If you can't solve your problem on the spot, ask to be taken to the nearest police station *(esquadra)*. To call the police in Lisbon, dial **346 6141** or **347 4730.**

Public notices. Here are some common signs you'll see:

Saída	Exit
Entrada	Entrance
Ocupado/Livre	Occupied/Free
Senhoras/Homens	Ladies/Men
É proibido fumar	No smoking
É proibida a entrada	No entry

English	Portuguese	Pronunciation
I don't feel well.	Não me sinto bem.	now muh SEE-too bay
Where is a drugstore?	Onde é que há uma farmácia?	O-duh eh keh ah OO-muh fuhr-MAH-syuh
I have	Estou com	ish-TOH ko ee-dee-zhuhsh-TOW
an upset stomach.	indigestão.	
I have an injury.	Estou ferido/-da.	ish-TOH fuh-REE-doo/-duh
toothache	dor de dentes	dohr duh DAY-teesh
headache	dor de cabeça	dohr duh kuh-BAY-suh
I feel pain…	Tenho uma dor…	TAY-nyoo OO-muh dohr
… in my leg	…na perna	nuh PEHR-nuh
… in my stomach	…no estômago	noo ish-TOH-muh-goo
… in my chest	…no peito	noo PAY-too
I am bleeding.	Estou a sangrar.	ish-TOH uh sa-GRAHR
I need a doctor.	Preciso de um médico.	pruh-SEE-zoo duh oo MEH-dee-koo
I feel dizzy.	Estou com tonturas.	ish-TOH ko to-TOO-ruhsh
Can you give me a prescription?	Pode-me passar uma receita?	POH-duh muh puh-SAHR OO-muh ruh-SAY-tuh
Help!	Socorro!	soo-KOH-roo
Stop thief!	Agarra que é ladrão!	uh-GAH-ruh kuh eh luh-DROW
Leave me alone.	Deixe-me em paz.	DAY-shuh muh ay pahsh
I've lost my wallet/passport.	Perdi a minha carteira/passaporte.	puhr-DEE uh MEE-nyuh kuhr-TAY-ruh/puh-suh-POHR-tuh
My credit cards have been stolen.	Roubaram-me os meus cartões de crédito.	roh-BAH-row muh oosh MEH-oosh kahr-TOYSH duh KREH-dee-too
I'm lost.	Estou perdido.	ish-TOH puhr-DEE-doo
Where's the police station/the hospital?	Onde é a esquadra/o hospital?	O-duh eh uh ehsh-KWAH-druh/oo ohsh-pee-TAHL
I have been assaulted.	Fui assaltado.	fooy uh-sahl-TAH-doo
witness/lawyer	testemunha/advogado	tuhsh-tuh-MOO-nyuh/uhd-voh-GAH-doo

THE PORTUGUESE WAY: INDEX

Signs Around Town:

Elevador	Elevator
Saldos	Sale
Caixa	Cashier
Empurre/Puxe	Push/Pull
Saída de emergência	Emergency exit
Peões	Pedestrians
S. f. f.	If you please *(Se faz favor)*
Atenção	Attention
Cuidado	Be careful
Avariado	Out of order

Useful Addresses and Phone Numbers in Lisbon

American Consulate: Avenida das Forças Armadas 1600 LISBOA
Phone: 726 6600

British Consulate: Rua da Estrela, 4, 1200 LISBOA, Phone: 395 4082

Canadian Consulate: Ed. MCB, Avenida da Liberdade, 144, 4º andar,
1200 LISBOA, Phone: 347 4892

South African Consulate: Avenida Luis Bivar, 10, 1097 LISBOA CODEX
Phone: 353 5041

Australian Embassy: Marqués Sa da Bandeira 8 r.c., 1050 LISBOA
Phone: 353-2555

Direcção-Geral do Turismo (Tourism Office)
Avenida António Augusto de Aguiar, 86, 1000 LISBOA
Phone: 57 50 86

JPM Publications SA • *Specialists in tailor-made guides*

12, avenue William-Fraisse, 1006 Lausanne, Switzerland
Copyright © 1994 JPM Publications SA – Printed in Switzerland

9/505